THE VIETNAMESE
EXPERIENCE
IN AMERICA

Minorities in Modern America

Editors
Warren F. Kimball
David Edwin Harrell, Jr.

THE VIETNAMESE EXPERIENCE IN AMERICA

PAUL JAMES RUTLEDGE

INDIANA UNIVERSITY PRESS

Bloomington and Indianapolis

The paper used in this publication meets the minimum requirements of American National Standard for Information Sciences—Permanence of Paper for Printed Library Materials, ANSI Z39.48-1984.

⊗™

Manufactured in the United States of America

Library of Congress Cataloging-in-Publication Data

Rutledge, Paul, date.
The Vietnamese experience in America / Paul James Rutledge.
p.   cm. — (Minorities in modern America)
Includes bibliographical references and index.
ISBN 0-253-34997-4 (cloth : alk. paper). — ISBN 0-253-20711-8 (pbk. : alk. paper)
1. Vietnamese Americans. I. Title. II. Series.
E184.V53R87 1992
973'.049592—dc20   91-26520

1 2 3 4 5   96 95 94 93 92

DEDICATION

There is a Vietnamese proverb which states, "An qua nho ke trong cay," or "When eating a fruit think of the person who planted the tree."

This book is the compilation of the experiences, hardships, and courage of Vietnamese refugee peoples who have come to America to begin a new life. To all who made and who continue to make that journey, this book is respectfully dedicated.

An man tra dao, "If one receives a plum, one must return a peach" . . . with appreciation for the plum.

CONTENTS

Illustrations follow chapter 4.

PREFACE

The rhetoric of commitment to world peace and human freedom espoused by world leaders notwithstanding, there is a growing number of dispossessed people in the world who have been, and are being, forced as a result of human cruelty and unconcern to seek refuge outside their country of birth. They seek refuge from political persecution, religious intolerance, economic deprivation, racial and ethnic discrimination, and/or military conflicts in their homeland.

Among these peoples are the Vietnamese refugees who began fleeing Vietnam following the fall of Saigon on April 30, 1975. At the time, their stories and the horrible reality of their desperate situation took the world stage by storm. Most forms of video and print media highlighted the mass exodus. The verbal and pictorial accounts that came out of South Vietnam mesmerized the world with unfathomable images of human misery and suffering. The struggle for freedom and survival was front page news.

Fifteen years later, Vietnamese refugees continue their struggle to survive, adapt, and establish futures for new generations of Vietnamese-Americans, but the spotlight of public attention has dimmed considerably. Unfortunately, in the intervening period the nations of our world have seen war, famine, religious civil conflict, lethal gassings, and innumerable atrocities perpetuated by the hands of one population against another. In the process, the relative calm of the Vietnamese-American adjustment into the American mosaic has often gone unnoticed.

Nevertheless, the sheer number of Vietnamese-Americans is beginning once again to draw the attention of the national media. The *Refugee News* in September 1989 reported that "approximately 75 percent of the total number of refugees who have been resettled in the U.S. since 1975 are from Southeast Asia (905,000)." *Time* magazine recently reported that "in San Jose bearers of the Vietnamese surname Nguyen outnumber the Joneses in the telephone directory 14 columns to eight" (April 9, 1990, p. 29), and in Oklahoma City, where the population of Vietnamese-Americans numbers approximately 10,000, a long-time Oklahoman of European ancestry remarked, "I don't know where all of these people came from, or when they got here, but they're here."

Within a few years of the arrival of the first waves of Vietnamese refugees, the leaders of Vietnamese-American communities crafted an adjustment strategy which maintained a relatively low profile in most of their local communities. Working to develop a strong foundation which would support the new arrivals, as well as subsequent arrivals, the Vietnamese remained in the shadows of the public vision. Their presence was known, but was certainly not overpowering. Now, stable and growing in influence both within Asian-American communities and within more Anglo-American communities, Vietnamese-Americans are initiating a more visible strategy and joining the multiracial variant we call America.

From the spotlight to the twilight, Vietnamese-Americans are now beginning to make their mark on the American future; and it is to our mutual benefit that they are moving out of the shadows.

ACKNOWLEDGMENTS

This book would not have been possible without the cooperation of Vietnamese-Americans with whom I have conversed for the past fifteen years in most of the fifty states. After conducting literally thousands of interviews, it would be impossible to thank all of the Vietnamese represented within these pages, but as I have shared the experiences of our newest Americans I have come to deeply appreciate their flight, their sense of life, and their resilience. I am indebted to each and all who over a period of years granted me the trust to know and hear their stories, and gain insight into their adjustment in the United States.

Out of respect for my friends, as well as professional ethics, I have granted the wish of those refugee people quoted in the book who asked not to be mentioned by name. Many of those interviewed were glad to be quoted, but for reasons which are apparent in the book, many were reticent. I have honored those requests, and wish to thank both the Vietnamese-Americans who were willing to speak by name, and also those who preferred to remain nameless but offer their understanding and have their stories told in something of an anonymous fashion. The combination is necessary in order to bring a fuller understanding of the Vietnamese experience both to and in America.

I would also like to thank my family. My wife, Suzanne, and my children, Jeremy and Maile, were always supportive and always willing to learn about and from our Vietnamese friends.

Numerous individuals have contributed to this work. Sue Bradford Edwards of the Department of Anthropology at the University of Missouri-St. Louis and Mary Hines, Administrative Associate in the Center for International Studies at the University of Missouri-St. Louis have assisted me through the typing of materials during the course of the writing. Kathryn

Jenson White, Assistant Professor of Journalism at Oklahoma Baptist University, and Ted West, a free lance photographer, graciously provided photo materials from their files, and the United Nations High Commission for Refugees has also provided materials from its research and public relations files. For the assistance which has been so graciously extended me, I acknowledge my indebtedness and my appreciation.

I am also appreciative to those who helped fund the necessary research carried out over many years in order to bring this work to fruition. The Center for International Studies at the University of Missouri-St. Louis, and its Director, Edwin H. Fedder, provided me with release time in order to write, and underwrote my final trip to corroborate materials and conduct further interviews in May and June of 1990. The Department of Anthropology at the University of Missouri-St. Louis has also assisted in funding short trips, and Van Reidhead, Chair, has worked effectively to help me juggle the time necessary to write, teach, and fulfill other duties. While teaching at Oklahoma Baptist University, from 1982 to 1989, the faculty development fund provided me with travel grants in 1983, 1984, 1986, and 1987, in order that I might travel and conduct necessary interviews.

I would also like to thank my friend Pham H. Quang, whom I first met in 1980, and who helped me with the language, provided insight into the culture of his people, and as an elder in the Buddhist community of Oklahoma, provided me access to materials and documents which have proven foundational to my understanding. It was Pham who also introduced me to the High Venerable One, the Buddhist priest with whom I have had numerous theological and personal conversations. Pham has always encouraged me and showed me the quality of friendship based on human sensitivity, not on race, nationality, or creed.

Most of all, I would like to thank the Vietnamese-American people. This is, after all, their story, their lives, and now their country.

THE VIETNAMESE
EXPERIENCE
IN AMERICA

I

THE VIETNAMESE ENTRANCE INTO AMERICA

The Fall of Saigon

With the dismantling of the American war machine in South Vietnam, the South Vietnamese Army was solely responsible for the protection of the country. Morale was low, supplies and recruits were lacking, and the fall of Saigon and therefore South Vietnam seemed inevitable. The approximately six thousand Americans still remaining in Vietnam in early 1975, the hundreds of thousands of Vietnamese who had fought in the South Vietnamese armed forces, and others who had worked against the north all feared for their lives once the North Vietnamese army established control over the South.

Signs of defeat for the noncommunist forces in Indochina had become evident with the mounting victories of the Khmer Rouge in Cambodia and the burgeoning strength of the North Vietnamese forces in Vietnam. These signs had precipitated plans by the United States refugee office within the State Department to prepare for the evacuation of American citizens and to inquire as to the potential willingness of Vietnam's neighbors to accept refugees. No one, however, was prepared for the massive nature of the refugee flight from Vietnam, Cambodia, and Laos or for the rapidity with which it began.[1]

After the fall of Saigon, on April 30, 1975, what had previously been a small stream of refugees quickly turned into a tidal wave. Within the first few weeks following Saigon's fall, an estimated 132,000 fled Vietnam. Many of those who left had fought alongside American forces, or served within the South Vietnamese government. They left by whatever means was available: U.S. military aircraft, U.S. Navy ships, small boats, on foot. To stay meant to die.[2]

The evacuation of Saigon was chaotic, poorly planned, and contributed to the panic of citizens seeking rescue. President Gerald Ford had stated that the United States had a plan for evacuating the Vietnamese from Saigon, and although this announcement came on April 10, prior to the fall of Saigon, the details of the plan were sketchy at best. The U.S. government had not considered the enormous need for evacuation, the numbers of Vietnamese who would want to be evacuated, or the exact numbers which would be allowed by the federal government to enter the United States.

Further convoluting the situation were the contradictory messages which emanated from the State Department. On April 15, Philip Habib of the State Department stated before the Senate Judiciary Committee's Subcommittee on Refugees and Escapees that the U.S. government was planning to evacuate from Saigon only U.S. citizens and a select number of Vietnamese, numbering approximately 17,600 persons, who were actually working for the U.S. government. Habib did not commit the State Department to assist persons whom the Department believed to be potential victims of the Northern army even though the State Department believed that the probability for mass murder was high.

Perhaps the reason for the unpreparedness of the State Department is found in their perception of timing. The resignation of Thieu, the disintegration of the South Vietnamese military forces, and the immediacy of refugee flight caught the Department by surprise. Ambassador Graham Martin, U.S. Secretary of Defense James Schlesinger, and others had full confidence in the South Vietnamese forces' ability, not to withstand the North indefinitely but at least to carry on the battle perhaps into 1976 before the fall would occur.[3]

When the end came, however, it came quickly. People began to flee in panic, and fear of one another, as well as of the opposing troops, permeated the evacuation as rumors spread throughout the region. One rumor was that the South Vietnamese forces might fire upon Americans in order to prevent them from leaving Saigon. Another story circulated that the Americans had already left and that no help would be forthcoming for any Vietnamese. Still another rumor persisted that the Ford administration had decided to abandon the evacuation attempt as too risky and would simply place all of the residents of Saigon at the mercy of the invading army.

In the circumstances of the moment, truth and rumor blended into one ambivalent fog and the result was a virtual stampede by persons desperate to leave the country. Supported by an attempt to organize an evacuation, and aided by friends within the U.S. armed forces, many Vietnamese were taken to U.S. ships by helicopters, boats, and ferries. Photographed and teletyped to the world, the flight from Saigon was beamed into living rooms around the world, and the nature of the situation became common knowledge. On April 17, Secretary of State Henry Kissinger personally communicated with Ambassador Martin and initiated a plan for evacuating not only American citizens, but also as many as 200,000 Vietnamese.[4] Discussions followed as to their destination. Originally the refugees were to be transported from Vietnam to neighboring Asian countries, but the plans were soon changed and they were taken to the United States following processing within designated camps or by specifically designated governmental personnel. While politicians debated the numbers, morality, and logistics of the mass movement of Vietnamese peoples, the Vietnamese fled.

The First and Second Waves of Refugees

Following the fall of Saigon, the first wave of Vietnamese refugees, estimated at approximately 132,000 people, left Vietnam seeking haven principally within the United States.[5] The characteristics of this first wave would prove to be distinctly different from subsequent waves of Vietnamese refugees. They were, by comparison, better educated, wealthier, and had political connections within the U.S. government. Many spoke English or at least had a working familiarity with the language. They included high-ranking soldiers, professional people who had worked with American personnel or companies in Vietnam, ethnic Vietnamese who had been educated within the United States educational system, and individuals who had family ties to America.

The first and second wave refugees were individuals and families who undoubtedly needed refuge in the United States. Their ties to the U.S. government and to the government of South Vietnam targeted them for extinction by the northern army and their admission to the United States was necessary for their survival.[6] Their need was visible and seemed obvious to the American government, and for many travel arrangements to the West had been negotiated prior to the fall of Saigon.

The first and second waves also contained "friends" of America. Subsequent waves of Vietnamese refugees would be looked on with disdain as fortune hunters, persons who were fleeing economic depression, but the first refugees were considered people to whom the country had something of a moral obligation. We had after all fought alongside the Vietnamese, and had not persevered in helping them win freedom for their country. Assisting them in relocation and allowing asylum in the United States was not only an obligation, it was also a means of dealing with the national guilt. Vietnam was viewed by many as the first war that America had ever lost. The first wave contained our allies in war and the families of allies who had lost their lives fighting in concert with American forces.

The first and second waves of refugees were different, also, in that they were easier to accommodate. With relatives in America, many of the refugees already had a place to go and the government was not responsible for their well-being. Wives of American servicemen and members of extended Vietnamese families already within America were much easier to process. They simply moved into established households.

Those with language skills were also initially easier to

assimilate into the American mosaic. Jobs were available for those who spoke English, even if those jobs were often less than desirable by American standards. In Houston, Vietnamese refugees often took jobs at local all-night convenience stores which had gone unfilled for months previously.[7] The jobs were low-paying positions, on the graveyard shift, in an area of high criminal activity. Nevertheless, they were, for some, an entrée to financial stability since they did not need to learn English.

The first wave also contained an unusually high percentage of Roman Catholics. These Vietnamese were more readily identified with American society since they were Christians.[8] This characteristic seemed to make them more acceptable and more understandable to many American citizens who used this point of identity as a catalyst for friendship.

The second wave of refugees began in approximately 1977. As a result of internal conflict, and renewed pressure by the Vietnamese government to expel ethnic Chinese peoples, including those who were citizens of Vietnam, thousands of persons fled to Thailand, Malaysia, Singapore, the Philippines, and Indonesia. Ethnic Chinese, Hmong, and other groups who had small representative numbers in the first wave, suddenly began to emerge in overwhelming numbers. The second wave is estimated at approximately 127,000 people although the documentation on the number fleeing Vietnam during this period is difficult to legitimize. Many of the second wave would eventually make their way to the United States.

One aspect of the refugee flow was now becoming clear. Several years after the fall of Saigon, there did not appear to be any end to the numbers of refugees attempting to leave the Southeast Asian peninsula. The first and second wave of refugees was the genesis of motion, but the current on the horizon indicated numerous waves yet to come.

Subsequent Waves of Refugee Peoples

The exodus from Vietnam continued with subsequent waves of people into the 1980s. Often these included many of

the ethnic minorities of Vietnam, who presented new problems for host countries and resettlement agencies depending
on the degree of acceptance which had been accorded them
on the Indochinese Peninsula. Migrating to the peninsula
over the centuries, they had settled into the countryside of
Vietnam but not always into the primary fabric of its society.
Among those ethnic minorities in subsequent waves were the
Cham, the Khmer, the Montagnards, and the Chinese.

The Cham were primarily congregated in the south-central
part of Vietnam. Numbering approximately 30,000 people,
they were fairly xenophobic in nature.[9] They were distin-
guishable in culture by the Hindu and Islamic influence evident in their religious practices and were often identified by
the Vietnamese with Malay peoples. This association with
peoples on the Malaysian peninsula often marked the Cham
for prejudicial treatment, and the regional prejudices have
carried over into Asian-American communities in the United
States.

The Montagnards comprised the second largest minority
group in Vietnam. They included more than thirty tribes, and
their estimated population was 800,000 prior to the escala-
tion of conflict in Vietnam. Montagnards (French for
"mountaineers") lived in the mountains of northern and central Vietnam. Essentially migratory, they practiced some
cultivation of rice and hunted the abundant animal life provided by the western high plateaus. During the Vietnam conflict, the Montagnards were often linked to the American
Central Intelligence Agency, and were suspected by the North
of being agents of the United States government.[10] Arguments have persisted as to the extent and degree of this
perception, but following the fall of Saigon, the Montagnards
were marked for annihilation by the North Vietnamese government. They fled to neighboring countries, and many then
came to the United States.

The Khmer people who live in and are associated with
Cambodia are also represented in Vietnamese society. Approximately 500,000 Khmer lived in Vietnam. They maintained their own language, religion, and cultural norms,
although many intermarried with ethnic Vietnamese people.

Most Khmer lived in the southern region of Vietnam around the Mekong Delta, and many became assimilated through the acquisition of Vietnamese citizenship and adoption of Vietnamese customs. Their interaction on a daily basis with mainstream Vietnamese society elevated them in the eyes of most Vietnamese above the Montagnards or the Cham, who were less well understood by the Vietnamese people. In the words of one Vietnamese man, "I knew lots of people who were not like us, but at least I had seen them. I knew that they were from Vietnam. I had only heard about Montagnards, and didn't really think of them like Vietnamese."

Numbering approximately 745,000 people, the ethnic Chinese in Vietnam have always played a major role in trade, economics, and merchandising.[11] Many had settled around the major cities of Saigon and Cholon around the turn of the century, and were heavily involved in exporting products to the rest of Southeast Asia. These Chinese merchants were well aware that if they did not flee when Saigon fell they would be vulnerable to the northern armies. Their properties and businesses would be confiscated, and their ability to survive economically would be destroyed. Coupled with this awareness was their fear of the Vietnamese with whom they did business. They had suffered persecution and harassment for decades (e.g., during the anti-Chinese riots in Saigon in 1919 and in Haiphong in 1927), and disliked the idea of having to reestablish themselves in a predominantly Vietnamese community overseas.

In an interview in Oklahoma City, a Vietnamese merchant corroborated this view:

> A Chinese [merchant] will cheat you. If he know[s] you are Vietnamese, he will charge you more. And if he know[s] that you are an American, he will charge you everything [as much as he can].
> I do not like the Chinese. They think they are better than Vietnamese. If I could, I would send them all back.

The subsequent waves of refugee people, then, not only included overwhelming numbers which demanded immediate attention by foreign governments, but brought with them the ethnic biases and prejudices which had been a part of life in Vietnam. The assumption that all of "these refugees" were essentially alike was erroneous. The culture clashes which had occurred in Vietnam were accentuated in the U.S. by the various groups competing for limited resources and assistance by international agencies and governments.

Refugees and Immigrants

In the light of world events, including the dismantling of Eastern Europe's communist political powers, the wars in Southeast Asia, and the questions posed by anticipated events including the return of Hong Kong in 1997 to the People's Republic of China, increasingly large numbers of people are leaving their country of origin and migrating to other lands. The exodus from Southeast Asia is now augmented by vast movements in Europe from Poland, Albania, and other Warsaw Pact nations, and the newly allowed immigration of Russian Jews to Israel. Refugees from Afghanistan, peoples from Southern Africa, and others who perceive themselves to be politically oppressed are looking to other countries for their future. In addition, persons from Ireland, Northern Africa, and Central America are moving across international boundaries looking for jobs and a better economic future. The disparity between the haves and have-nots is increasing in many nations around the world, and the ability to rebound from natural disasters is a near impossibility in most of the poorer countries. Conflicts between ethnic and religious groups in India, Sri Lanka, Ireland, and across Southern Asia are intensifying, and the outlook for peace given the history of these conflicts is not promising.

Given these world situations and increasing populations of third world nations, population movements will continue and grow for the foreseeable future. The number of those crossing national borders is staggering, and the ability of nations to respond to human need is limited, necessitating some form of political categorization in an effort to determine who may or may not enter one's country.

Alien populations are generally defined by a fourfold taxonomic system. They are refugees, migrants, asylum seekers, or haven seekers. Refugees according to the *Refugee and Immigrant Resource Directory* are persons who are outside their country of nationality and who are unwilling to return because of persecution or anticipated persecution.[12] The persecution may be based on race, religion, nationality, membership in a particular social category, or political allegiance.

Migrants are generally alien workers, and depending on the country into which they are migrating, they may be legal or illegal. Oftentimes they are seasonal, returning to their country following a harvest or the cessation of a job. Asylum seekers are defined ambivalently by the U.S. government as those persons who are in the process of being designated as either migrant, immigrant, or refugee, while haven seekers are those who are seeking a temporary haven from danger in their country of origin.[13]

Politically the difference among the four categories is significant. There are limitations on the number of immigrants who may enter the United States from any one country in any given year. Refugees, however, are exempt from numerical quotas, and may enter the United States without regard to population figures. They are permitted to reside in the United States for one year and following the twelve-month adjustment period are allowed to apply for citizenship.[14] Technically, refugees are considered nonimmigrants and are not calculated in the data gathered by the Immigration and Naturalization Service used to control the flow of nationals into the United States.

A significant factor in the Vietnamese flight from their homeland is the fact that they left as refugees and not as immigrants. This not only facilitates their entrance in America, but it also reveals a substantial portion of the trauma experienced in their move from Vietnam to the United States.

Immigrants are persons who migrate from one geographical location to another on a voluntary basis (personal choice), and who, prior to that migration, have a destination in mind.[15] Usually the trip is well planned, and is a single journey involving short but safe stops along the way.

A refugee undertakes a forced migration toward an unknown destination and oftentimes has numerous stops en route. There is little if any time to prepare, and the traumatic experiences imposed upon persons through various archipelago routes are generally not anticipated. Kunz's theory of refugee flight shows that once the initial flight has been set in motion, the refugee movement is shaped not by internal but rather by external forces acting upon it.[16]

As refugees, the Vietnamese were an acute movement, not an anticipatory one. Anticipatory movements foresee a need to move, and have enough lead time to prepare for resettlement in an orderly fashion. Refugees of acute movements are normally coerced into leaving through powerful military or political opponents and in a need to escape a given situation move quickly without the benefit of preparation. Therefore, in the moment of danger, fleeing becomes the best possible solution. This response, however, normally results in regret at having left one's homeland and frequently the desire to return remains strong.

The hurried nature of the refugees' departure also explains to a large degree why so many refugees from Vietnam choose to emigrate to America. During the war, first and second wave refugees had developed ties to persons in the United States and they fully expected and received assistance in their flight from their homeland from military and political friends. Some Vietnamese would have preferred to stay in Asia, but the options for relocation in most Asian countries were simply not available. Realizing that they were not welcome in neighboring countries, and with limited choices made in an extremely brief period under crisis circumstances, the Vietnamese chose the path to America through the ambivalence of preference and default. It seemed at once both the best and the only plausible choice.

Designated as refugees, Vietnamese peoples have been permitted to enter America in unusually large numbers in a relatively short period of time. This has on the one hand facilitated their need for haven and relocation, and on the other raised questions about U.S. policy regarding refugees and all people seeking to permanently relocate in the United States. The caring capacity of the land, the government, and the American people have all been brought into question as the flow of refugees continues to swell.

From the Vietnamese perspective, refugee status is necessary for quick movement out of Vietnam, and for expediting the bringing of family members out of Southeast Asia to America once a portion of the family has arrived and settled in a local community. As one Vietnamese man, now living in Southern California, stated, "We are all refugees. I did not leave my country by choice. I was forced to leave. I am glad to have my new home here, but I did not [originally] plan to come here. I had to leave my country or die."

The Countries of First Asylum

The nearest points of safety for the Vietnamese who were forced to flee their homeland were eastern Thailand and the shores of Malaysia bordering the South China Sea. Neither Thailand nor Malaysia had "volunteered" to be countries of first asylum; it was a matter of geographical default. The influx of refugees in need of food, medical care, shelter, and the other necessities of life burdened economies which were not prepared to support unlimited numbers for indefinite periods. Nevertheless, beginning in 1975, they came.

The initial response of both countries was humanitarian and compassionate, but the massive numbers of refugees so overburdened their economies that even with the assistance of such international agencies as the United Nations, Red Cross (in Thailand), the Red Crescent (in Malaysia), and various other volunteer organizations from Canada, Australia, and the United States, their hospitality soon wore thin. Malaysia refused to accept any more refugees as of 1979, and has held to this policy. Thailand, which has assisted over one million refugees since 1975, is continuing to do what it can but is distressed at the West's diminishing interest in the problem.[17]

Indonesia, geographically the largest country in Southeast Asia, was not initially a major relocation point for Vietnamese refugees, but it temporarily became one after Thailand and Malaysia curtailed their efforts, at least for ethnic Vietnamese. Currently, Indonesia's government identifies all refugees as economic migrants and as such they are turned away.[18]

Hong Kong, with its population of approximately 5.5 million people crowded into a land area of less than 400 square miles, has diligently tried to discourage refugees by making itself as unattractive as possible as a housing and/or staging area but has been relatively unsuccessful. With the restrictive policies of other first asylum countries, Hong Kong became the only viable alternative for refugees. As of 1982, it has identified all refugees as illegal immigrants and either refused them entry or processed them and resettled them in other countries. Since 1978, more than 110,000 have entered, but over 80 percent of these have since been resettled elsewhere.[19]

The Countries of Second Asylum

Singapore, with one of the most tightly controlled immigration policies in all of Southeast Asia, with rare exception turns all Vietnamese refugees away. Given its small area and already dense population, this is perhaps understandable. In 1978, it set a quota maximizing the number of refugees in Singapore at 1,000 and limiting the stay of any one refugee to 90 days.[20]

The Philippines, on the other hand, is one of the largest staging areas for refugees. Large numbers waiting for resettlement in the West are brought there for final processing and placement. At processing centers administered by the Philippine Ministry of Human Settlements, the United States, and the U.N. High Commission for Refugees, individuals and families are reviewed for resettlement and given instruction in the language of their host country and in cross-cultural communication. The National Council of

Churches and the Red Cross have also been active in helping with the camps, as have some Filipino volunteer groups.[21]

Macau, about forty miles from Hong Kong, is administered by the Portuguese government as an overseas province. Vietnamese refugees there number fewer than 500, and the government refuses to accept any additional persons, even on a temporary basis, actively directing boatloads of refugees to Hong Kong despite that government's formal objections.[22]

The policy of the People's Republic of China has been exactly the opposite. It grants permanent asylum to almost every refugee who arrives there and requests it. Relatively few have done so, since most refugees find China about as desirable as Vietnam. The vast majority who did have been of Chinese descent and so were able to adjust with some rapidity. They have been placed in work cooperatives and encouraged to become self-sufficient as quickly as possible.[23]

Japan has cooperated in the refugee assistance program since 1977, and then only because of world pressure. It spent several years formulating a policy, and only in April of 1979 did it approve the entrance of Vietnamese refugees into Japan with a ceiling of 500 persons. That ceiling was later increased to 3,000, most of whom the Japanese government was diligently seeking to relocate elsewhere. Japan has also donated money to the UNHCR, the World Food Program, the Red Cross, and other international agencies, and has sent physicians, nutritionists, and other workers to camps elsewhere in Southeast Asia. On the whole, Japan has given major financial help to care-givers in other nations, but has settled only a relatively small number of refugees—an insignificant contribution to the total picture.[24]

Today, refugees claiming to be fleeing from persecution are being met with growing disbelief. Many are viewed as simply fleeing from poverty or hoping for prosperity and as such are not defined as refugees. The problem is compounded by assistance fatigue on the part of care-givers. Western nations are increasingly raising barriers against refugee entrance, although requests for asylum continue.

Indochinese Refugee Movements since 1975
(as of September 30, 1988)

	Sept. 1988 population	Arrivals since 4/75	Reductions since 4/75				
			To U.S.	To other countries	Vol. repat.	Relo-cation	Other
Hong Kong	25,010	147,963	50,153	60,239	26	0	273
Macau	465	7,659	2,427	3,514	0	0	574
Indonesia	2,118	104,055	42,600	40,423	6	0	49
Malaysia	12,467	235,118	88,120	92,458	8	0	136
Philippines	5,217	45,620	9,978	14,745	9	0	36
Singapore	345	33,630	5,583	19,950	1	0	3
Other	807	41,375	6,231	33,307	0	0	15
Thailand—Khmer	17,340*	239,216	50,357	72,969	42	41,172	261
Thailand—Highlanders	54,069*	158,619	52,883	21,535	748	0	2,448
Thailand—Lao	17,817*	191,379	71,960	45,161	2,523	1,000	3,227
Thailand—Vietnamese Land	601*	31,458	8,052	12,028	0	0	178
Thailand—Vietnamese Boat	12,324*	103,550	28,003	26,603	2	0	292
SUBTOTAL Thailand only	102,151*	724,222	221,255	178,296	3,315	42,172	6,406
SUBTOTAL Land Refugees	89,827	620,688	183,252	151,694	3,313	42,172	6,114
SUBTOTAL Boat Refugees	58,753	718,954	233,095	291,238	52	0	1,378
TOTAL	148,580	1,339,642	416,347	442,932	3,365	42,172	7,492

Source: Adapted from *The Bridge*, December 1988, pg. 13.

II

EMIGRATION TO THE UNITED STATES

The Flight

The initial flight from Vietnam began under desperate conditions. When Vietnamese individuals and families sought to escape their country, their immediate concern was to flee dangers which threatened their lives. As is characteristic of persons in acute situations, the Vietnamese in their desire to protect themselves focused on leaving, and often did not anticipate the obstacles which they would encounter during the flight from Vietnam.

The trip out of Vietnam to a haven of safety had difficulties of its own. Most of the refugees did not know where they were headed, and many were not aware of the distances or the hardships involved. Reacting to events around them, as opposed to planning one's migration carefully as most immigrants have the opportunity to do, created enormous stress and frustration as the refugees became lost, were separated from one another, and found that provisions hastily made generally did not suffice.

Individuals who had connections with American military personnel or American government officials had the easiest time. Air transportation was dispatched to help selected individuals and their families leave the country, and for those persons the primary necessities were provided aboard American military vessels once they were safely off shore. Even those who received assistance, however, were seldom sure of their final location, and were dependent on the military to escort them to a place of the military's choosing.

Refugees who fled in small fishing boats or who walked overland suffered severe hardships. Food and water were in short supply. Bandits and small gangs preyed on the helpless, and robberies occurred frequently. The North Vietnamese forces routinely shelled groups of "Southern sympathizers," and the Khmer Rouge was not reticent about murdering Vietnamese when they were discovered escaping along the pedestrian paths through Cambodia. Pirates overtook the boats in the South China Sea and the Gulf of Thailand, and the overcrowded conditions on many of the boats caused them to sink. There is no way of knowing how many were killed during their attempts to flee.

An added hardship not envisioned by refugees was the death of so many friends and countrymen. Seeing people die of hunger, shot in an attempt to flee bandits, or blown to pieces when stepping unsuspectingly on unexploded ordinance was an almost daily experience. In the memory of one Vietnamese mother, this was the most stressful fear of all:

> I saw people die of hunger, and I could not help them. I did not know if I would die also so I saved my food for my daughter [six years old at the time of flight].
>
> I was afraid to let her walk very far because I saw people who had lost legs, or had eyes lost by things [explosives] they stepped on. I carried my daughter until I was exhausted and then I asked my sister for help. Every step made us afraid. I didn't know what to do. If we went back we would die, so we just kept going forward hearing stories all of the time about others who had made it okay. We tried not to think about it a lot, but it was all around us and we couldn't get it out of our heads.

Experiences in Transit

The flight from Vietnam to countries of first asylum proved to be fraught with danger and horrors both physical and psychological. The experiences of refugees are hard to comprehend for one who has not undergone such a traumatic displacement. The possibility of success was often marginal and there is no record of how many refugees died at sea, during the land marches, or at the hands of bandits or pirates. Even for those who were successful, nightmares linger; the psychological aftermath of their experiences continues to haunt them.

The experiences of the refugees come more fully alive in their own stories and in their own words.[1] The following accounts are from persons who made the perilous journey from Vietnam and who presently live in the United States.

Mai

Mai was born in Saigon and was fourteen at the time she and her family left Vietnam. Her father had served in the South Vietnamese military and her mother felt certain that all of the family would be marked for destruction once the North had instituted their governmental control in the South.

So Mai and her family sought to escape. They and approximately eighty other people crowded aboard a small fishing boat and headed out into the South China Sea, hoping to be rescued by an American naval vessel. They had been at sea for about three days when they were intercepted by what Mai thought was either a Malaysian or a Thai fishing boat.

> I did not know [at first] that these were pirates. But one of them grabbed me and forced me onto their boat along with some of the other girls. Four men took me into the boat [below the deck] and raped me over and over again. I tried to fight them, but they only beat me and laughed at me.

For the next four days, nine different Thai men repeatedly raped and beat the young Vietnamese women. They were terrorized with verbal threats, thrust at with knives, and forced to perform sexual acts which frightened and humiliated them. One of the refugee women was so frightened that she froze and did not comply with the pirates' demands. In their attempt to coerce her into submission, the pirates bludgeoned her to death and then dumped her body into the sea.

After several days of raiding other small refugee boats, the pirates had new victims and grew tired of Mai and her companions. She and her friends were then thrown overboard into the South China Sea and forced to try and survive until someone else came along. During the hours that Mai treaded water and prayed, she lost sight of most of the other young women. After an undetermined time, a boat of refugees spotted her and took her and one other young women aboard. She does not know if the others who were thrown overboard were lucky enough to survive.

Soon

Soon is a Vietnamese woman born in the vicinity of Bienhoa in South Vietnam. She arrived in the United States in 1979, after a series of refugee camp experiences, and now lives in central Oklahoma.

Soon lived on a farm in South Vietnam, and the rumors and realities of war had been a part of her life as long as she can remember. When the American army first arrived, her family met and decided that two of her sons should join the South Vietnamese army. The expectation for military service among the men of her community was very high, and although she did not completely share this feeling, she knew that her sons would eventually join the conflict in support of their country. She had seen the results of war and in the process had lost her naiveté.

> I had seen children without arms and babies who were killed by the land bombs. Sometimes the babies were in their mothers' arms when they were killed. I did not always know who was doing this or why, but after a while it did not seem to matter. Too many friends did not come back [from the war], and I did not want to lose my sons, too.

Years later when it was apparent that the war was lost, Soon and her family made plans to escape Vietnam. By this time, one of her sons had been killed in the war, and she had not heard from the other for more than a year. The family cautioned one another not to discuss their escape plans even with the closest neighbors since they felt that no one could be fully trusted. The communists had infiltrated the villages and hamlets with individuals who were constantly providing information to the North Vietnamese Army and loyalties, even of friends, were in doubt.

Soon and her family left in the middle of the night. They took only what they could carry and hurried on foot toward the Cambodian border. They hoped to reach the border, find temporary shelter in Cambodia, and then make plans for the future.

The walk to Cambodia was longer than they had envisioned, and more difficult. They met thousands of refugees along the road and heard about boats which were taking refugees out to American ships for passage to the United States. They had to be cautious about pickpockets and bandits, and guarded their food constantly. In Soon's party were seven people including her youngest son, her grandson, three daughters, and her daughter-in-law.

After fourteen days of travel, they arrived at the site which had been described to them as a good place to find passage on a boat. There were several private fishing boats and the owners who were also fleeing Vietnam offered to take passengers who could pay them for the privilege. The owners were anxious to leave and Soon remembers the shouting and shoving as people argued with the owners about getting a place on the boats. Since most of the people had no money, bartering with the owners to accept food, religious articles, or other forms of payment was common. Frightened and panicky, she was surprised when she learned that she had been given a place on one of the more substantial boats which was leaving the following day. She did not know at the time, but would later discover, that the passage had been secured with the sexual favors of two of her daughters. They had offered themselves to the captain and his helper in exchange for transporting the family members out of Cambodia.

Soon had expected that the journey would take only a few hours. She was aware that the boat was overcrowded but the owner assured the people that an American vessel would rescue them once they were out of sight of the shore and in international waters.

The American ship which was promised was never found and instead Soon and the other refugees spent six days at sea. By the third day, the escapees were lost and the boat was simply drifting. During this period, they were attacked twice by Thai pirates and on both occasions several people were killed and several women were raped. What few belongings the refugees had were stolen by the pirates and on the fifth day when the second attack occurred, five young girls and three young boys were taken away by the pirates. The fate of these eight young people can only be imagined, and Soon did not hear about them again.

Land was finally sighted on the sixth day and the Vietnamese attempted to land on the Malaysian coast. It was difficult to manuever the boat to shore and they could see the remains of other boats which had not been able to navigate through the channels to the beach.

Approximately seventy-five yards from shore, many people began to jump overboard attempting to swim ashore. Some were swamped by the waves, but many made it. Upon reaching land, the Vietnamese were stunned to find a large group of people who were throwing rocks and stones at them forcing them back into the water. Some were armed with knives, and the Vietnamese who had reached the shore turned about and swam toward the boat again. Some of these were caught in the current and drowned, and those who did survive were even more confused and frightened than before.

They continued to drift down the shoreline; following two more failed attempts at landing, they were located and assisted by Malaysian government officials who spotted their boat floundering in the waves. These officials had been alerted to the influx of refugees and they had established small camps to assist those who were rescued from the sea. Soon and her family were glad to have survived, and of all of the good things which met her on shore, she said the best was fresh water.

Tran

Tran was a Vietnamese soldier who had served in the army for several years prior to the fall of Saigon. In April 1975 he was still enlisted in the army, and at the time was attached to a headquarters unit with both American and South Vietnamese personnel. He had many friends in the American group and they proved to be most supportive in his flight from Vietnam.

> I left Vietnam by boat, and headed to Hong Kong. I was helped by Americans who gave me American money to buy my ticket so that I could more easily escape Saigon. The ship I was on was a strong one, and I reached Hong Kong in five days. When I got to Hong Kong, I had an American sponsor which my [American] army friends had arranged for me. Since I already knew English, and since I had letters from my friends who were going back to live in the states, I did not have a hard time getting to America. I was very lucky.

When Tran arrived in the United States, he was provided with a place to live by his American friends and given a job in the community. He worked for three years in a grocery store as a helper while receiving free rent in a duplex in exchange for maintenance of the house and yard. During these three years, he managed to bring his fiancée and her parents to America, save some money to purchase a house of his own, and make plans for a secondary move within the continental United States. Today, Tran lives in Seattle with his wife, her parents, and their two children.

Loc

Loc was nine years old when his family began their flight from Vietnam. They left one evening under the cover of darkness, traveling on foot and carrying with them most of their valuables. After the first night, they were stopped by Vietnamese troops who took their money and most of their food and interrogated them.

> The soldiers made me sit by myself away from my father. I was afraid and this one soldier kept looking at me. He would come over and act like he was going to hit me, but he never did.
> I had been sitting alone for two hours when the soldier in

charge came over and asked me if we had any gold with us. When I told him "no" he hit me with his fist and told me to tell the truth. He hit me three times and then placed his pistol barrel on my stomach and said that he was going to shoot me if I didn't tell him where the gold was hidden. I cried and could not talk. The soldier spit on me and walked away.

Later during the night, the soldiers told us to leave. We all got up as fast as we could from our sleep and left. They let us take some of our food and clothes with us but kept a lot of our things. All of us had been beaten but everybody was still alive.

Loc and his family finally made it to the Cambodian border. Their trip would continue into Thailand where they were accepted into a refugee camp and where for two and a half years they waited for resettlement. During that time, one of his sisters died and his father became very ill. Finally, they were moved to another camp, processed by American officials, and permitted to immigrate into the United States. Today, Loc lives in Southern California where he is enrolled in a community college while working two jobs to help support his extended family.

Pham

Pham was born and reared in Saigon. When the communists first took over South Vietnam Pham did not try to escape, believing that all Vietnamese could live together peacefully.

The communists told us that they would treat us well. I thought that they would do as they said, but I was very wrong. I was placed in a job working hard but the communists did not pay me enough to live. They kept telling us that we were traitors and that we had betrayed the real Vietnamese people. They told us that they should kill us but that they were being good to us by letting us work in their land. We were told that the consequence for helping the enemy was that we lost our country. Maybe we could earn the right to be Vietnamese again some day, but now we were just dogs.

Pham decided to escape in early 1977. On his first attempt, he was caught and imprisoned. He remained incarcerated for three months before he was released and returned to his job. Following his return the authorities watched him closely and although he continued to look for ways to leave it would be almost two years before he could successfully escape.

Like many Vietnamese, Pham bought his passage out of Vietnam. He bribed a Vietnamese government worker who told him of a boat which was leaving Vietnam and who offered him a ride along with several other men to where the boat was moored. When he got there, he found that the boat was too crowded, but no one wanted to be left behind. There was a total of almost two hundred people who huddled together and pushed the boat out into the sea. Most of the people stood or lay asleep from exhaustion on each other. Food was available for the first day but quickly ran out. Water was at a premium, and so it was given only to the children and the pregnant women. Many of the passengers became seasick, and the stench of vomit permeated the boat.

> People prayed because we thought that we would die. Some people had died, and we knew that if we were not picked up soon [by a passing ship] we would die, because we had run out of water.

Pham lost track of time. The heat of the sun combined with the swelling of the ocean waves kept the passengers fatigued trying to cope with the weather. It was hot during the day, and cold in the evening wind. The skin on Pham's hands and arms begin to crack and he cut his shirt into strips covering different parts of his exposed body from time to time trying to regulate the solar burns. He had lost a lot of weight, and spent as much time as he could sleeping. He wanted to reserve his energy and fight the boredom.

One of the men saw something on the horizon. They did not know where they were since they had been drifting for some time and some feared that it might be a communist patrol boat. As it sailed closer, it was unmistakably a very large ship and Pham along with the others on the boat begin to yell, hoping that it was not a communist boat but realizing that they would die soon without help.

My eyes were hurting from the salt and I could not see the ship
very well. People in front of me were crying and I heard a
woman say that it was an American ship. I could not see for
myself and I just prayed that she was right.

The ship proved to be part of the American Navy, and
subsequently rescued the refugees. They were given food and
medical aid, and then turned over to refugee officials of the
United Nations. They were assigned to closed camps and
ultimately resettled in the West.

Hue

Hue and his family left Vietnam in October 1978. His father
bribed several government workers over a period of eighteen
months in order to gain permission to leave the country. They
left on a boat which was loaded by government soldiers who
in turn demanded gold before the trawler could leave Vietnam. The soldiers outfitted the boat with provisions, a
searchlight, and a hastily drawn map showing the route to
Malaysia.

The trip to Malaysia took just under three days. While en
route the trawler passed a ship flying an American flag and
the refugees shouted for help. Hue was close enough that he
could see the deckhands leaning on the rails pointing at their
boat, but except for gesturing in their direction it did not
acknowledge them in any way. Later on the same day, they
saw a ship with a flag he did not recognize, but when they
shouted at the sailors they were waved away and the ship
refused to stop.

Although the trip took only three days, it seemed forever to
Hue. The water ran out quickly, and after the middle of the
second day it was rationed. Each person was allowed only
one swallow of water when they were thirsty. Some of the
older people died, and because the boat was so crowded, the
bodies were lowered over the side and prayers were said for
them as they were buried in the ocean.

When the trawler did arrive in Malaysia the captain had to
pay the Malay people to let the Vietnamese disembark. It was
evident that the captain had brought groups to this location

before, but even so he argued vehemently with the Malay officials over the price for unloading his human cargo. Before Hue and his family could leave the boat, they had to give the captain more money and leave with him the few oranges they had left among them. Others on the boat were also forced to surrender many of their valuables to the captain or were threatened with return to Vietnam.

Once in Malaysia, the refugees were directed to a holding center. They were given lodging in a shelter which had been built as temporary housing for refugee people. It had walls on two sides, a ceiling, and was approximately one hundred square feet in size. Within the shelter were three families with seventeen family members among them.

> I remember that we had so many people in the camp and no privacy. There were no toilets, and we had to find a coconut tree or walk out on a long pier and use the ocean as our toilet.
> There were only Vietnamese people in the compound, and some Malay guards who didn't talk to us. We had to wait in long lines for interviews but we wanted to get out and we had nothing else to do. Medicine was not given to us even when my mother became very sick. The Malays kept telling us that the medicine was on its way, but we never got any.

Hue and his family spent only eight months in the camp. They were interviewed, processed for resettlement in the West, and moved to Hong Kong in a relatively short time. In Hong Kong, since they had an American sponsor, they spent only four days waiting for a flight to the United States, and today live in the Midwest where the family runs a Chinese-Vietnamese restaurant.

Trinh

Prior to the fall of Saigon, Trinh was a local businessman in Saigon. He did not have time to liquidate his holdings before the communist takeover and remained in Vietnam hoping to continue operating his business under the communist government. On May 16, 1975, Trinh was arrested for treason and his business was confiscated by government troops. He was

taken to a reeducation camp where he was told that he must
be cleansed of his capitalist thinking.

> I was made to do hard labor and listen to lectures every day. I
> was told that I was a criminal who had cheated the people and
> that I must be made to pay for my crimes against the state and
> against the people. I knew that I had not cheated anyone but I
> had to agree if I wanted to get out of the camps.

After two years in the reeducation facility, Trinh was told
that he would be released if he would address the inmates of
the camp and confess his crimes. He had confessed on four
previous occasions, but the camp administration had continuously accused him of insincerity. To assure the leaders of
his honesty, he was also instructed to give a presentation of
the virtues of communism and the priorities of the state over
the family. Trinh, who was a practicing Buddhist and who
believed in the family loyalty system taught through Confucianism, knew that he must be convincing in his testimony
or he would not be dismissed from the camp.

> I was told that I could talk to the other prisoners only after the
> leaders had approved my speech. They told me that I was a
> liar and that the Americans had poisoned me. I was afraid
> that they could see through what I had prepared to say, but
> somehow they were convinced. I spoke for two hours denounc-
> ing America, my fellow traitors in Vietnam, and begging
> forgiveness for my awful crimes. I did not believe one thing
> that I said, but I learned that I can be a good actor if it is
> [that], or die.

Trinh was released from the compound three weeks later
and returned to his home neighborhood. His business had
been taken over by the state, was run by government employees, and he was forbidden from going on the premises. He
had decided long ago while in the reeducation camp to leave
Vietnam and now he was sure that there was nothing left for
him there. Two days after his return to Saigon, he began his
trek through Cambodia into Thailand and eventually made
his escape to the West.

Van

Van is a middle-aged man who has had more than one experience fleeing from the communist regimes of Vietnam. In 1951, when he was a teenager, his family fled North Vietnam due to the persecution by the communist government of Roman Catholics. As Roman Catholics, his family was active in the village church, and Van's younger brothers and sisters were enrolled in catechism classes. When the communists gained control over his province, they closed the church and imprisoned the priest. Rumors persisted that the priest had been murdered and the family decided to move to the southern region of Vietnam.

Twenty-five years later, Van found himself fleeing the communists once again. Fearing similar persecution under a new communist government in the south, Van evacuated Vietnam with the help of friends in the South Vietnamese government. They were able to secure him and his family a place on a ship destined for Hong Kong. Van's trip was not as horrible as the trips of many of his countrypeople, but the refugee camp experience he recounts was extremely unpleasant.

> I thought that we would be housed in fairly clean and comfortable quarters. Since I had a high-ranking position, I was treated better than most, but even that was inadequate. There was not enough rice for our family, and the water tasted bad.
>
> I thought that the people [officials] of the camp were rude. They were always in a rush, and we could not get the information we needed. I was always being put off, and I was able to get the help I needed only because I knew some people [in the government].
>
> The hours of waiting were the worst. I missed my country and I could only imagine what the communists were doing to our friends and neighbors. I tried to find out about friends of ours, but no one had any information. Not knowing was the hardest part of all.
>
> No, realizing that I could never go back was the hardest.

Van and his family, because of their contacts in the United States, did not stay in the camps for very long. It was long enough, however, to convince Van that he needed to assist as many Vietnamese as possible in accomplishing resettlement in the shortest period of time. His experience has led him to be very active in his city's Vietnamese Mutual Assistance Association and he has personally sponsored several families in their relocation to the United States and Canada.

Bao

Bao was a Buddhist priest in South Vietnam and a proponent of peace. He had led peace marches in the South, and had encouraged his own government to negotiate with the North. He had worked to bring greater harmony between Buddhists and Catholics in South Vietnam and believed that all peoples could coexist peacefully in love and mutual respect. With these beliefs foundational to his perspective on life, Bao was shocked at the behavior of the conquering troops.

> I was surprised when I went out to meet the soldiers that they threatened me with their weapons. The first soldier I met struck me across the face with his rifle, and spit on me as I lay in the street. I stood up and held out to him a gesture of peace, but he walked away laughing and cursing. A [fellow] priest not far from where I was standing was shot, and he died before we [could] get him to the hospital.

Bao watched helplessly as soldiers tore apart the temple he held sacred. They riddled the statue of the Buddha with machine gun fire and slashed the altar cloths with their bayonets, screaming profanity at the priests. Bao was told to squat in a corner of the temple and soldiers took turns urinating on him as he sat motionless.

> I did not think that soldiers fighting for a cause which they said would help all people would treat our temple with such disrespect. I had heard stories but there had been so many rumors about the North, that I did not put much faith in the stories. I believe that Buddhism is a part of every heart, and so I did not think that the communists would try to destroy our religion and our sacred temple. I knew that it would be diffi-

cult to convince the new rulers that Buddhism should play a role in governing the new Vietnam, but I thought that they would at least let us live [coexist as an institution].

Bao was taken to a holding area where there were educators, local politicians, and other priests. In the midst of his horror, he was reminded by other captives that he had painted the North Vietnamese as reasonable; people who only wanted to have a united Vietnam ruled by all of the Vietnamese people. He had not envisioned himself or his faith as an enemy of anyone, much less of any other Vietnamese. It was at this point that Bao entered what he terms as a deep state of depression. In order to combat his sense of futility and his grievous misjudgments, Bao meditated on the basic teachings of Mahayana Buddhism. He remembered the rules of the *sangha* (Buddhist religious order), thought back over the years of his service to the Buddha, and mentally recalled the Buddha's teachings.

> It was my memories of the festivals which kept me alive. The times of celebration in the pagoda and the religious meaning of those times kept the fire of hope burning inside of me. It was those memories, too, which made me know that I must escape this new government which would not let me follow the teachings of my religion or seek the Buddha-nature.

Bao was one of only two monks who survived the destruction of the temple where he served, and the only one of the two who had reached the United States as of early 1990. His escape was made possible by several Vietnamese who still remain in Vietnam and for that reason he does not want to discuss the details of his flight. He not only lectures in Buddhist temples in the United States, but volunteers his time to speak at public gatherings in order to inform Americans about the continued need for assisting refugees from Southeast Asia.

Trac

Trac is a senior in high school and recently became an American citizen. He was born south of Saigon, and he and his four aunts, one brother, and one uncle escaped by boat from Vietnam when he was a small child.

> My aunt saw a government ship checking around looking for people but they did not see us. We had turned out our lights. We were stranded on the ocean for ten days before being rescued by some Thai fishermen. We later stayed in a Malaysian camp for one year, but I was so young I do not remember a lot about it.

Trac did not leave Vietnam with his parents. Shortly before his departure his father was arrested by the government for assisting other people in escaping from Vietnam, and Trac's mother chose to remain behind in order to help her husband. Trac's father died in prison and two years after his arrival in the United States Trac was reunited with his mother. She had fled Vietnam alone and made her way through the refugee camps to Canada and finally to the United States. They presently live in central Oklahoma with the four aunts and one uncle with whom he originally escaped.

Hua

Hua was twenty years old when his family quit Vietnam. Hua refers to his departure as quitting the country, because they knew that they could not live under the communists' rule. He was fortunate in that his family were wealthy, and were able to accumulate sufficient funds for their travel. They paid approximately $800 American for a share in a boat which was to take 502 people from Vietnam to Malaysia.

They left for Malaysia from Ca Mau and promptly encountered the Vietnamese coast guard. Through conversations and monetary payoffs, the group was not only permitted to pass, but was actually escorted out of Vietnam's territorial waters. The boat was overloaded; it was designed to carry only about two-thirds of the weight which it bore. Hua constantly feared that the boat would sink or that it would be an easy target for Thai pirates.

On the third day the passengers ran out of water. The captain, who thought he had stored enough for a ten-day voyage, did not anticipate people using the water for washing out their mouths and bathing. Conservation of the water supply became a priority and the captain changed his original route so that they could land a day earlier than originally planned in Malaysia. The new route meant that they spotted the Malaysian shore on the fourth day but the landing site was already saturated with Vietnamese refugees. Landing was prohibited by naval vessels who gave Hua and the others fresh water and then forced them back out to sea.

The captain turned the boat toward Indonesia and steered for what he believed was the closest port. About forty hours later an American offshore oil derrick came into view and the boat stopped to ask for help. "The people on the platform were really nice to us. They gave us food and let us sleep there for the night so we wouldn't get lost in the darkness. The next morning they gave us fresh fruit and showed us the direction of Indonesia."

The following day Hua and the other refugees landed on the Indonesian island of Letuu. The residents of the island did not want the refugees to settle permanently but offered to let them stay for about a week and rest from their experience. After seven days, the authorities of Letuu transported the refugees to Airrea where they could make contact with American Peace Corps workers.

The Peace Corps aided the refugees in resettling. Rice rations were provided and temporary shelter was available. The refugee population of Airrea had reached more than 15,000, and the local inhabitants were growing nervous about the size of the refugee community. Quarrels between the Vietnamese and the Indonesians broke out over prices for foodstuffs in the local markets, and animosities between the two groups began to grow. The problem became so unmanageable and the threat of impending violence so evident that the Indonesian government sent in military personnel to quiet the situation. An uneasy peace ensued for the next several weeks, during which time Hua was processed for resettlement in the United States.

Following the normal procedures of interviews, Hua and his family, having now been selected for resettlement, left

Indonesia and flew to Singapore. For the first time, Hua felt reluctance about moving to America. He thought that perhaps his family would be better suited to Singapore. "The house we stayed in was beautiful. It had clean, running water, and television. It had electrical things [appliances] which I had never seen before. It was too good to be true. I didn't think America could be any better than that."

Singapore was not an option for Hua and his family and they proceeded with their plans to live in America. Eleven months after arriving in Singapore, they boarded a plane for California where they were met by relatives and driven to Kansas. Today the family lives in two adjacent houses and shares the responsibility of running a Vietnamese supermarket and butcher shop.

Entry and Orientation

With the flight from Vietnam behind them and the camp experience now a memory, Vietnamese refugees arriving in America often believed that the major problems had been overcome. Their principal worry had been acceptance for resettlement in America, not the adjustments to the American way of life which might follow. Even though they had sat through classes on American society and cultures, they did not foresee the process of adjustment as being difficult.

Therefore, it was a surprise for many refugees that their first stop in America was another refugee camp. Camp Pendleton in California, Fort Chaffee in Arkansas, Eglin Air Force Base in Florida, and Indiantown Gap in Pennsylvania were receiving centers for refugees arriving in the United States, but these camps did not parallel the camps in Southeast Asia. In most of the camps, conditions were not ideal but were vastly improved over their counterparts in Asia. Serving as more of a temporary home than a transient outpost, the American camps provided food, clean water, medical care, recreation, mailing privileges, daycare, libraries, education (usually the teaching of English), and religious services both Buddhist and Roman Catholic. Knowing that this was the last stop prior to full entry into American society, the mental health of the refugees improved tremendously and sagging spirits revived.

Having completed the physical journey from Southeast Asia to America, the refugees now turned their attention to problems of relocation. Most refugees experienced some degree of culture shock although the degree and extent varied considerably, usually determined at least partially by the preconceived myths which the refugee held about America and the American people—misconceptions which produced erroneous expectations of life in America.

The adjustment to the American mosaic came when most refugees were still struggling with the magnitude of expulsion from their homeland. Ideas about customs, manners, behavioral expectations—which many thought they understood because they had met or knew an American in Vietnam—proved on more than one occasion to be inaccurate. The first glimpse of these misunderstandings usually surfaced in the sponsorship program when the Vietnamese families came into contact with individual families, religious organizations, or community agencies who were their resettlement sponsors. The cultural miscommunications underscored in a graphic manner the enormous undertaking inherent in adjusting to a secondary culture.

This adjustment was apparent in the misconception held by refugees that all Americans are wealthy. Homes with televisions, stoves, microwaves, and two cars symbolized great wealth to many of the refugee people. Americans dressed well, had indoor heating and air conditioning, and some of the American children even had their own telephones. As a Vietnamese woman newly arrived in America for only five weeks remarked,

> All Americans have lots of money. The children have money in [their] pockets, and can buy without [their] parents' permission. I sometimes wonder where the money comes from. I think that the government must give all Americans so much money since they have so much they must not use.

The apparent financial strength of middle income Americans, who provided the bulk of individual support in sponsoring Vietnamese refugees, sometimes caused difficulty for the refugees and for their sponsors. The rumor persisted within American refugee camps that the government paid a stipend directly to the sponsoring family which the sponsors were to give to the refugees. Although there was no truth to the rumor that the sponsors were channels for government payments to the refugees, many refugees believed it and were upset when the cash assistance was not forthcoming.

> I had risked my life to get to America and I was not able to bring with me my life's things. When I got here, your country gave my sponsor money for me but they spent it on themselves. When I complained they said that they did not have any money from the government for me but they would help me apply for the money. But I knew that the government would not send my money to them and me, too, so I did not bother to go down there [to the governmental office to apply]. [Vietnamese man, Oklahoma City]
>
> To be honest, I don't think the family we helped really appreciated it. We had to dip into our savings and we were glad to do it, but we would have liked to have been treated more graciously by the [Vietnamese] family. They just seemed to take it for granted and expect more. [Sponsoring family, Midwest city, Oklahoma]

The adjustment process for refugees and for sponsoring groups thus proved far more difficult than originally estimated. Humanitarian concerns notwithstanding, even genuine expressions of human kindness were misconstrued and the message sent was somehow distorted in the behavioral transmission. Becoming oriented to another culture and society took far longer and was exceedingly more difficult than most of the refugee people had anticipated. Insight into that process is revealed in the comment of a Vietnamese grocer in Fort Worth, Texas: "I worked for Americans in Vietnam, and I had visited America once. But I am [still] having a hard time understanding you Americans. I like you, but I do not understand why you do some things."

III

INITIAL RESETTLEMENT

U.S. Resettlement Policies

Since the days of the English colonies on the Eastern sea-board, what was to become the United States of America has been populated by immigrants from other lands. The Native Americans who are indigenous to North America were numerically overcome by European immigrants in just a few decades, and Anglo arrivals would later be rivaled by mass influxes of Asian workers. America has become renowned as a place of refuge for persons seeking freedom and asylum from persecution.

The history of the United States is replete with immigration, but in spite of that history, definitive statutes on immigration and refugee admissions have never been formulated. No one within the government has direct constitutional power to control immigration and Congress's authority is "subject to limited judicial scrutiny."[1] Prior to the Southeast Asian exodus in 1975, refugees entering the United States came by one of three avenues. Special temporary legislation allowed huge numbers of refugees into the United States following World War II, bypassing existing quotas on immigrants as a response to the war's end. The Immigration and Nationality Act of 1952 reaffirmed a national origins system, set limits on immigration, and provided for a conditional entry provision for several thousand refugees who did not qualify under the other guidelines of the act. When the act of 1952 proved to be inadequate, the Attorney General's office exercised its power over refugee entrants, and in 1965 the

Immigration and Nationality Act abolished the national origins system and in its place instituted annual ceilings on countries.

The exodus from Indochina and the growing numbers of refugees from Afghanistan, Poland, and Central America made a specific act for refugees necessary so that the United States could regulate admissions into the country. In 1980, the Refugee Act was passed, superseding the Immigration and Nationality Act in the area of refugees and defining a process for refugee entrance and resettlement. It defined under U.S. law who is a refugee and who may be admitted under refugee status, closely paralleling the definition employed by the United Nations Convention on the Status of Refugees. The Refugee Act of 1980, Section 201, defines a refugee as "any person who is outside any country of such person's nationality or, in the case of a person having no nationality, is outside any country in which such a person last habitually resided, and who is unable or unwilling to return to, and is unable or unwilling to avail himself or herself of the protection of that country because of persecution or a well-founded fear of persecution on account of race, religion, nationality, membership in a particular social group, or political opinion."[2]

Refugees and Asylees Granted Lawful
Permanent Resident Status
from Vietnam, Fiscal Years 1946–1987

Year(s)	Number
1946–50	—
1951–60	2
1961–70	7
1971–80	150,266
1981–87	260,626
TOTAL	410,901

Source: 1987 Statistical Yearbook of the Immigration and Naturalization Service

Southeast Asian Refugee Arrivals in the United States

Resettled under Special Parole Program (1975)	129,792
Resettled under Humanitarian Parole Program (1975)	602
Resettled under Special Lao Program (1976)	3,466
Resettled under Expanded Parole Program (1976)	11,000
Resettled under "Boat Cases" Program as of August 1, 1977	1,883
Resettled under Indochinese Parole Programs:	
August 1, 1977–September 30, 1977	680
October 1, 1977–September 30, 1978	20,397
October 1, 1978–September 30, 1979	80,678
October 1, 1979–September 30, 1980	166,727
Resettled under Refugee Act of 1980:	
October 1, 1980–September 30, 1981	132,454
October 1, 1981–September 30, 1982	72,155
October 1, 1982–September 30, 1983	39,167
October 1, 1983–September 30, 1984	52,000
October 1, 1984–September 30, 1985	49,853
October 1, 1985–September 30, 1986	45,391
October 1, 1986–September 30, 1987	40,164
October 1, 1987–September 30, 1988	35,083
October 1, 1988–September 30, 1989	37,066
TOTAL	**918,558**

Prior to the passage of the Refugee Act of 1980, most Southeast Asian refugees entered the United States as "parolees" (refugees) under a series of parole authorizations granted by the Attorney General under the Immigration and Nationality Act. These parole authorizations are usually identified by the terms used in this table.

Source: Office of Refugee Resettlement

Four federal agencies were charged with responsibility for applying the new act. These were the Office of the United States Coordinator for Refugee Affairs (USCRA), the Bureau for Refugee Programs (BRP) under the U.S. State Department, the Office of Refugee Resettlement (ORR) under the Department of Health and Human Services (DHHS), and the Immigration and Naturalization Service (INS). The U.S.

Coordinator for Refugee Affairs has primary responsibility for coordinating refugee policy in the U.S. USCRA does not have operational authority and is entrusted with a mediating function between and among public and private refugee assistance agencies. The BRP oversees the development and maintenance of relief policies conducted overseas representing the U.S. government in internationally orchestrated relief programs as they are administered by volunteer groups or national governments.

The Office of Refugee Resettlement has been given the task of administrating the domestic assistance program. It serves as a clearing house for information on refugees, assists state officials with refugee needs and problems, and provides cash assistance, social services, and a broad range of refugee programs which enhance resettlement success. The actual processing of refugees, including determination of refugee status of an individual or family for entry into the United States, is the job of the Immigration and Naturalization Service.

State governments also play an important role in the nation's resettlement policies. It is the states who regulate cash assistance programs, often serving as funnels for federal money. They provide guidelines for volunteer groups within their jurisdiction and many offer contracts to private businesses who teach English and/or give guidance and employment counseling. The volunteer groups serve as contact persons working directly with the refugees in the implementation of programs beginning in overseas assistance, working alongside public officials in the American camps, and following through on the local level as the refugees settle into a given community.

The policy of the United States government also includes the use of those perhaps best equipped to assist refugees in their adjustment to American society: other refugees. Mutual Assistance Associations (MAA), sometimes named the Vietnamese-American Association of a particular city, are composed of refugees who are already settled and who have formed a network to help new arrivals[3]. MAAs offer language services and interpreters, practical courses on how to drive a car or shop in the local supermarket, employment services,

Southeast Asian Refugees: Estimated Cumulative State
Populations[a]—Including Entries from 1975 through 9/30/89

State of Residence	Estimated Total	State of Residence	Estimated Total
Alabama	3,400	Nevada	2,500
Alaska	200	New Hampshire	900
Arizona	7,600	New Jersey	8,400
Arkansas	3,200	New Mexico	2,300
California	363,800	New York	33,100
Colorado	12,400	North Carolina	6,900
Connecticut	8,200	North Dakota	1,000
Delaware	300	Ohio	12,600
District of Columbia	1,800	Oklahoma	9,200
Florida	15,700	Oregon	20,500
Georgia	1,200	Pennsylvania	29,200
Hawaii	7,900	Rhode Island	7,600
Idaho	1,900	South Carolina	2,500
Illinois	29,300	South Dakota	1,100
Indiana	4,400	Tennessee	6,300
Iowa	10,200	Texas	68,400
Kansas	10,800	Utah	9,200
Kentucky	3,100	Vermont	700
Louisiana	15,300	Virginia	23,100
Maine	1,700	Washington	43,000
Maryland	10,800	West Virginia	400
Massachusetts	29,500	Wisconsin	15,300
Michigan	12,500	Wyoming	200
Minnesota	33,800	Guam	300
Mississippi	1,900	Other Territories	[b]
Missouri	8,400		
Montana	1,000	TOTAL	918,500
Nebraska	0		

[a]Adjusted for secondary migration through 9/30/89, rounded to the nearest hundred. Not adjusted for births and deaths in the U.S.
[b]Fewer than 100.
Source: Department of Health and Human Services, Office of Refugee Resettlement.

conomic advice and assistance on a limited basis, and information on aspects of Vietnamese culture in the local community which would be of interest to new arrivals. Pamphlets on customs, how to shop, and where to go for medical needs are all prominently displayed, and volunteers help to acclimate the incoming refugees to their new social environment.

The policy of the United States government actively seeks to use all of the human resources into which it can tap. Beginning on the federal level and moving down through the state and local levels, it encourages participation by assistance groups both public and private. Funding is direct from the central government, indirect through the states, and supportive through grants to both volunteer agencies and Mutual Assistance Associations. The essential prerequisite for funding is the ability to meet the definition of a refugee as delineated in the Refugee Act of 1980.

Community Reception

The initial reception by communities across America to the influx of Vietnamese refugees was positive. Predicated by guilt from a losing war effort and spurred by humanitarian concern, communities made preparations for welcoming refugees into the country. Religious agencies such as the Roman Catholic Social Agency, the Lutheran Church, the Southern Baptist Convention, and the Church World Service Organization designated funds, rallied supporters, trained volunteers, and renovated old houses as they anticipated the refugees' arrival. Local businesses and groups of war veterans contributed to community chests to aid refugees, and a spirit of helpfulness generally abounded.

One example of this reception in 1975 shortly after the fall of South Vietnam is provided by the Kailua Baptist Church located on Windward Oahu, in Hawaii. The congregation was composed of Anglo, Asian, and Black members some of whom had fought in Vietnam. A few of the members had ties to Vietnam, but most had never visited Southeast Asia.

As the fall of Saigon became imminent, the church voted to

assist financially and personally in helping refugees who were coming to Hawaii. People volunteered their homes for temporary shelter, and food, clothing, and material goods were collected for distribution. A communications center was established in the church office, and persons within the community who were not a part of the church were encouraged to participate as well. Anyone who had a skill or an interest was invited to join in the effort.

One of the obvious needs was for language instruction. Conversational English classes were organized, and teachers began to prepare for teaching English as a second language. The Vietnamese Immigrant Volunteer Assistance Committee of Hawaii (VIVA) targeted the church as an agency to which they would refer people for literacy training. On May 25, 1975, the church began its first language classes with an evening enrollment of 163 people.[4]

But the size of the refugee population and subsequently the needs of the refugee community had been underestimated by the church. By June, approximately 2,500 people from Vietnam had arrived in Hawaii with more than 1,600 temporarily residing in Kailua. The resources of a congregation which numbered about 300 in its worship attendance were quickly depleted, and partners were sought for continuation of the programs. One of the members, Charles Farr, a vice president of American Factors, Inc. (AMFAC), a large conglomerate based in the islands, was instrumental in securing support from his company. AMFAC donated $500 and unlimited use of their duplicating equipment and agreed to encourage other companies to contribute. With this gift as a springboard, the pattern for community-wide support had been laid, and was maintained as the refugees moved through Hawaii to the American mainland.

Collective altruism, then, was the hallmark of those initial years. Sponsors stepped forward and were mobilized, and refugees were assigned to both individual and group sponsors. The rescue psychology throughout America was strong, and the perception that lives were saved and a partial debt payment was being made to the Vietnamese people permeated the resettlement effort. This mentality persisted for years but gradually begin to play itself out as communities became fatigued in both their efforts and their desire to help the endless flow of human beings.

Community Conflict

Unfortunately, positive community reception was not the only response to Vietnamese refugees. Due perhaps to the volume and suddenness of their arrival, the sentiment against the imbalance of imports from Asia generally, the misunderstanding that the arriving Vietnamese were Communists, and a generalized growing anti-immigrant attitude among some Americans, the refugees also encountered resistance and prejudice, some of it passive as in the boycotting of Asian stores, and some of it active and violent.

Some of the most extreme reactions to the refugees' presence were exhibited on the Gulf coast of Texas. Between Galveston and Corpus Christi Vietnamese shrimpers worked the gulf alongside more traditional Texas shrimpers. Their inadvertent violation of unwritten rules of territoriality combined with a decline in the price of shrimp positioned the Vietnamese as scapegoats for the shrimpers' anger. In 1980, in Seabrook, Texas, local shrimpers burned several refugee fishing boats. Confrontations over the incident resulted in the killing of an American shrimper by two refugee men. Later acquitted by a Texas jury for having acted in self-defense, the Vietnamese were nevertheless held responsible by the fishing community.[5]

Other burnings and confrontations ensued. In April 1981, a group of Vietnamese fishermen asked a federal judge to help them find protection against the Ku Klux Klan after two boats were burned and several families were threatened with violence. Klan members, hooded and armed with high-powered rifles, rowed boats into the Gulf acting as a vigilante patrol. Crosses and replicas of boats were torched in the yards of Vietnamese residents, and the Klan gave the Vietnamese four weeks to pack their belongings and leave.[6]

In New Orleans, refugees and fishermen exchanged rifle

fire over rights to a local fishing area. In Biloxi, Mississippi, fist fights broke out between Vietnamese shrimpers and local captains, and the local shrimp industry printed and sold bumper stickers that read, "Save Your Shrimp Industry: Get Rid of Vietnamese, Contact Your Local Congressman."[7] The fishermen were angered by the Vietnamese use of illegal nets such as a gillnets, made of clear monofilament and anchored on the ocean floor, which they believed overfished the area resulting in a market glut lowering the price of their catch. In California, nets were cut into pieces both on shore and at sea, and tensions escalated. The California Department of Fish and Game, the Mutual Assistance Association, and the U.S. Coast Guard pooled their resources and commenced classes for Vietnamese refugees on fishing laws, procedure, and etiquette.[8]

The attempt to enculturate Vietnamese shrimpers met with positive results. Vietnamese who previously did not understand the American dislike of boat contact no longer allowed their boats to bump American ones either when they were moored or while in the process of fishing.[9] Conversations between the antagonists were arranged, and with increased communication the problems began to dissipate. Mutual respect based on a strong work ethic developed and the Vietnamese and locals sought to compliment what they admired about each other. One Galveston fisherman remarked, "They [Vietnamese] do work hard. You have to give them that, and now that we give them the rules I think that it will work out."

Not all misunderstandings were reconciled so amicably, and many have not been reconciled at all. In Oklahoma City, residents of a local neighborhood resented the locating of a Vietnamese Buddhist temple in one of the houses adjacent to their property. Obscene gestures and racial remarks were thrown at the communicants in hopes that they would move to another part of the city. Three members were approached by four men and threatened with a baseball bat. In an interview conducted in 1982, one Anglo resident expressed his views in the following manner: "We don't need these chinks around here screwing up our kids. There are places where they can go but it ain't here. If I wanted some un-American fish-eater in my neighborhood, I'd go kill the bastard and plant him in the backyard."

Violence did rear its ugly head in places besides the Gulf Coast. In May 1990 in New York City, a gang of black men attacked a group of Vietnamese, thinking they were Korean. The men were angry about a local Korean-American store which they were boycotting and which they believed to be prejudiced toward blacks. One of the Vietnamese youths was beaten with a baseball bat and all were subjected to racial slurs.[10]

The most visible tragedy occurred on January 17, 1989, in the schoolyard of the Cleveland Elementary School in Stockton, California. As students were assembling to return to their classrooms, a man walked onto the playground and opened fire with a AK-47 assault rifle. Five children were murdered, and twenty-nine other children and one teacher were wounded. The five dead included four children from Cambodia: Ram Chun, Sokhim An, Rathanar Or, and Oeun Lim; and one child from Vietnam: Tran Thanh Thuy. Most of the other casualties were refugee children from Vietnam, Cambodia, and Laos.

The Stockton community and the Stockton Southeast Asian refugees immediately banded together to provide support for the victims and their families. A Southeast Asian Community Development Foundation refugee scholarship fund was established in memory of those who died, and residents quickly dispelled any perceptions of collusion in the tragedy. Stockton was genuinely horrified, and the sensitivity of longtime residents toward the refugee families cohesively bound culturally diverse peoples together. As a result of this community-shared nightmare, the Stockton Southeast Asian Community has established the following three goals for its organization: (1) educate the community at large about refugees from Vietnam, Cambodia, and Laos; (2) build bridges that assist and empower the Southeast Asian community itself; (3) enhance among the broad populace a greater understanding of the Southeast Asian cause.[11]

Vietnamese Culture in America

When the Vietnamese refugees left Vietnam they left their country of birth but they did not abandon their indigenous culture. Patterns of thinking, methods of behaving, and standards whereby one is measured as acceptable or unacceptable are all parts of one's cultural inheritance and therefore part of oneself. As the Vietnamese adjusted to America, Americans also adjusted to the Vietnamese, and discovered them to be unique and in many ways distinctive from Japanese-Americans and Chinese-Americans. To better understand Vietnamese-Americans, it is helpful to understand basic elements of the Vietnamese culture and the Vietnamese character as self-ascribed by the refugees themselves.

The Vietnamese view themselves historically, and presently, as harmony-oriented. To the maximum degree possible, Vietnamese people desire to bring peace to other people, and to respond to them in the way that bring them the most joy. The Taoist philosophical concept of harmony is practiced by many refugee people, and sometimes this leads to cross-cultural confusion.

> My sponsor asked me to go to his church, but I cannot go [because] I am a Buddhist. I could not also say "no" because I do not want to be ungrateful for all his help. So I say "yes" to make him feel good and know that I like him. When I did not go, he called and was upset, but he did not say why. [Refugee man, Dallas, Texas]

Vietnamese have been described as eclectic, adaptable, resourceful, practical, passive, indirect, and resilient. All of these modifiers are appropriate from a Western point of view, but when you inquire of Vietnamese, they describe themselves as hard-working or industrious. They speak of themselves as *"tran can cu"* and believe that it is a part of the national character. The concept of *"tran can cu"* combines hard work, patience, and tenacity into a relentless drive to survive or be successful.

The Vietnamese self-perception also includes humility,[12] a

virtue which some Vietnamese believe is misunderstood as
weakness by Americans. Americans revere rugged individualism, and are often uncomfortable in the presence of self-
effacing Vietnamese.

> I should never think of myself first or better [than anyone
> else]. That is hard for my American friends who think that
> winning is being better. Being better is working together so
> that everybody wins. Nobody wins alone. No one [alone]
> should take credit for victory. [Vietnamese Buddhist, New
> Orleans]

Vietnamese do value achievement and accomplishments, and
generally speaking are highly motivated to excel. The idea of
humility does not preclude self-determination and individual
or collective advancement.

The Vietnamese philosophical outlook on life differs little
from that of many middle-class Americans and for that reason they have adapted well into the American mainstream.
They value the family and see it as the lynchpin of society.
Parents and persons of advanced age are to be respected, and
education is primary. Religion is to be revered, and the views
of all people respected. Respect for all life is taught, and
tolerance for cultural preferences which run counter to their
own is a part of that respectful expression toward others.
Living in harmony, extending peace to all life, and allowing
for the fulfillment of one's life in the manner of one's personal
choosing distinctively mark the societal concepts of Vietnamese refugee people.

> I cannot tell you what you [should] to do with your life. I care
> that you are not in pain, but I do not tell you [what to do].
> Your fate and choices will tell you that. [Vietnamese elder,
> Tulsa]

All of these characteristics are part of a dynamic, living,
albeit changing and adapting, Vietnamese culture in America—a culture which brings with it aspects of the old country
and which is now beginning to incorporate influences from
the new homeland.

Vietnamese Religious Life

The beliefs of various religious systems, and the practice of religion, exert a deep influence on the Vietnamese refugee people. The religious thought of many Vietnamese has been a blending of a number of systems, choosing not to claim one and denounce the others but rather to mix the teachings of various faiths in order to meet the particular needs of their community or family. This syncretistic practice is deeply rooted in the practice of religion by Vietnamese people. That is not to say that they do not espouse one primary religion; in fact, there is usually an umbrella religion under which the others are subsumed.

Although most Vietnamese are Buddhist, either by practice or claim, Vietnamese refugees in America also ascribe to Confucianism, Taoism, Roman Catholicism, and a variety of Eastern religions less well known in the West. Culturally, all of the refugees have been influenced by "The Three Teachings." These teachings have permeated Vietnamese customs, manners, and social structure and constitute a trinitarian philosophy emerging from the blending of Buddhist theories of reincarnation and the law of moral retribution, the Taoist metaphysical concept of harmony, and Confucianist ethical and social principles for the family and for government.

Buddhism was introduced into Vietnam by traders from India and China. The Chinese brought with them Mahayana Buddhism, or the Greater Vehicle, and the Indians brought with them Theravada Buddhism, or the Lesser Vehicle. Mahayana Buddhism had the greater effect and the conversion to Buddhism via the Mahayanist School runs historically concurrent with the overwhelming influence of China on Vietnam. India's influence was minimal at best, while China's mark on Vietnam was significant enough that Vietnam has been referred to as the "Lesser Dragon." A minority of Vietnamese Buddhists practice Theravada Buddhism, also known as Hinayana Buddhism, but the majority, over 93 percent, practice Mahayana Buddhism.[13]

One of the primary features of Buddhism which affects

Buddhist culture and adjustment into the United States is the concept of the Middle Path to salvation. This belief colors the way in which all of life is viewed, and to a large degree influences everyday behavior. The ideas are called "The Four Noble Truths" and are as follows: (1) existence (life) is suffering, all life is suffering; (2) suffering is caused by inherently insatiable desires; everyone has these desires; (3) desire must be suppressed in order to end suffering; (4) desire is suppressed when one adheres to the Eightfold Path. The Eightfold Path entails right speech, right action, right livelihood, right views, right intentions, self-discipline, self-mastery, and contemplation.[14] These eight areas provide guidelines for personal interaction, social organization, and almost every area of one's cultural frame of reference.

Confucianism is considered by many scholars to be a religious philosophy rather than a religion per se, but behaviorally speaking, there is no question about its tremendous impact on Vietnamese culture and society. Confucianism was introduced into Vietnam around the eleventh century, addressing itself to the maintenance of social and family order. For K'ung Fu Zu, better known in the West as Confucius, the ethical standards from which all of life flowed are *Jen*, benevolence or altruism; *Shu*, tolerance and reciprocity; and *Hsiao*, respect and obedience, which manifested itself in the practice of filial piety.[15] The ranking of society and the family structured for Confucianists the proper order of things. The four classes of society were historically the intelligentsia, the peasants, the craftsmen, and the merchants, who were on the bottom of the ladder. One was to honor the king, the teacher, and the father in a prescribed hierarchical pattern.

The greatest contribution to social organization, however, was to be found within the family. Ideal harmony, taught Master Kung, rode upon the expression of filial piety. Filial piety is a hierarchical relationship where the subordinate pays proper allegiance and respect to his or her superior. These relationships, always moving in a unidirectional linear line, are those *embodied in relationships* involving son to father, wife to husband, younger brother to elder brother, servant to master, and citizen to emperor. The last of these has been adapted over the years to imply proper respect from friend to friend, and to construct for adherents behavioral standards both within the home as well as within society at large. In the scriptures of Confucianism, the heart of appropriate behavior is summed up in Lun Yu 15:23, "What you do not want done to yourself, do not do to others."[16]

Taoism is another of the many outside religions to enter Vietnam although it was never as fully embraced as was Buddhism or Confucianism. The principle teachings are charity to all living things, simplicity of life, patience, contentment, and harmony among people and between humans and nature. In an excellent example of syncretism, many Buddhists, for instance, have incorporated aspects of Taoism into their belief and practice but do not claim to be Taoists.

In the sixteenth century, Portuguese Christian missionaries arrived in Vietnam and were later followed by the Spanish and French, bringing with them Roman Catholicism. The faith spread rapidly among Vietnamese in the seventeenth and eighteenth centuries. Numbering approximately 10 percent of Vietnam's population, Roman Catholics are nevertheless disproportionately represented among the Vietnamese refugees in the United States.[17] Figures vary, but it is estimated that as many as 29 to 40 percent of the refugee people in America are Roman Catholic.[18]

Other religious perspectives are represented by smaller groups of Vietnamese refugees, but continue to determine behavior and therefore adjustment inclinations. The Cao-Dai or *Dai Dao Tam Ky Pho Do* (Third Amnesty of God) combines Buddhism, Confucianism, Taoism, and Roman Catholicism.[19] Theologically an enigma to many purists, members genuflect before the statue of the Buddhist and burn incense to Mother Mary. Important to adaptation, however, is the fact that in Vietnam they were politically active and staunchly anti-Communist, features which would normally identify them solidly with other Vietnamese refugees except for their theological stance. It is their doctrine which makes them unwelcome to most Vietnamese, and which excludes them from a public profession of their affiliation or from participation within developing Vietnamese communities.

Phat giao hoa-Hao, or Hoa-Hao, began in Vietnam in 1939 and is exclusively a movement relegated to the Mekong Delta area. Unlike Cao-Dai, Hoa-Hao does not blend multiple religions into one but rather emphasizes a highly disciplined personal prayer life. It has no temples or formal liturgies, but has grown steadily into a religion with more than one and one-half million worshippers in Vietnam.[20]

Religious sects are also found within the refugee community. Len Dong, a spirit cult, emphasizes the possession of women mediums called *ba dong,* who become a catalyst for communicating with one's ancestors or other spirits. Tam Giao, the Three Ways, is the actual and formalized practice of the Three Teachings mentioned earlier and is practiced by both Roman Catholics and Protestants. Ancestor veneration is viewed differently by almost everyone but is understood to mean the creation at the ancestor altar of an invisible world in which one may worship or show appreciation using whatever particular religion he or she chooses.

Religious buildings and services have become an important part of the refugee community. They are both centers for assisting refugees and community gathering places. They are a visible symbol to many Vietnamese that they are an integral part of America and that they are accepted while maintaining their own cultural identity. In Port Arthur, Texas, the Vietnamese population has its own grocery stores, insurance agents, beauty parlors, and a Vietnamese temple and religious park. The Vietnamese community purchased a Baptist church building and renovated it to create a Buddhist temple. In 1987, Mayor Malcolm Clark assisted at the dedication of the temple in which a large number of Texans participated.[21]

The religion of the Vietnamese in Port Arthur has introduced new elements into the community. In early 1988, the Port Arthur Vietnamese Community Association requested that the local school district grant a public holiday for the celebration of Têt. Têt is the Vietnamese New Year and to many Vietnamese Buddhists and Catholics it has strong religious significance. For a southeast Texas petroleum town, this was a new idea indeed, but it warranted investigation since 1,000 of the district's 9,000 students were Vietnamese. In a spirit of cooperation and in a decision reflecting the growth of the refugee community, the school board decided not to create a district-wide holiday, but to grant excused absences to Vietnamese children who were celebrating Têt either as a cultural or religious holiday.

These compromises and adaptations normally fall within the domain of the Vietnamese community. In Oklahoma City, local residents were worried about the Buddhist pagoda and what might be taking place inside the temple grounds:

> I do not like them practicing that funny religion. I know there's going to be some trouble down there if they keep that up [meeting for worship in the temple]. I just don't like people down there doing funny stuff. [Anglo woman, thirty-four years old, Oklahoma City]

To counter misconceptions, the Buddhist Association devised an active strategy to win support within the neighborhood. One of the three monks who lived in a house behind the pagoda went door to door and introduced himself to the residents. He introduced himself as "Tony," spoke good English, and invited the children to free martial arts classes to be held in the temple building. At the first meeting of the class, the monk stood out front wearing bluejeans, greeting the children and their parents, and cooking hot dogs over an open grill. To many of the residents, the cultural chasm was narrowed considerably.

> I didn't know they were so much like us. They were even friendly, and so I told David that he could stay and even go back. I guess being in America has really helped them. [Donna, twenty-nine years old, mother of David, age nine]

Additional adaptations were undertaken by the Buddhist Association. Desiring to be perceived as truly American, they changed their name from Buddhist Temple to Buddhist Church. They sang songs which from outside the church building sounded like traditional Christian hymns even though they were in Vietnamese and not English. One such song was "Jesus Loves Me," with the substitution of Buddha for Jesus. Given the tune, one would assume that the song is Christian, but in Vietnamese the lyrics said, "Buddha loves me, this I know, for the sutras tell me so."[22]

The Buddhist group bought pews from a Methodist church. When the front doors were opened wide the interior gave every appearance of a typical Protestant sanctuary. When the doors were closed, the pews were moved to the side of the room, the Buddha which had been covered with a curtain was uncovered and placed in the center of the room, and the worshippers sat on the floor for the program of meditation and worship. When interviewed, Buddhist leaders stated that their desire was not to deceive people, but to be accepted.

> We try to adapt and to be like Americans. But we also want to keep our culture, I mean part of our culture at least, because this is what helps us remember we are Vietnamese, too. [Vietnamese Buddhist monk]

> I love America and I love my religion. I am glad that I am both. To be an American is to be free and to be a Vietnamese is to be Buddhist. That is why I am both. That way I have two cultures. [Vietnamese grandmother, Buddhist temple, Oklahoma City]

Other aspects of the Buddhist religion identify for people their heritage, culture, and their value system. Dr. Dao T. Xuong, President of the Vietnamese Buddhist Association of Oklahoma, commented to the religious editor of the *Saturday Oklahoman and Times*, in January 1981, that Buddhist celebrations enable refugees "to get together and remember old times." Nguyen Anh speaks of the strength she finds in Buddhist symbols: "When I go to the temple I see the Buddhist flag and each of the colors remind me of what I [am] to be as a Vietnamese." The High Venerable One, Thich Giac Nhien, explained that each of the colors in the Buddhist flag marks a characteristic of Vietnamese Buddhists and shows what all people should be. The colors were adopted by the

Buddhist Convention in Sri Lanka in 1947 and represent these qualities: blue, wisdom; red, progress; yellow, compassion; white, charity; orange, purity.[23]

Not everyone sees these religions as positive, and expressions of frustration are not uncommon. Sister Anne of Oklahoma City, who works with teenagers through the auspices of the Roman Catholic Diocese, worries that the people have a "tendency to withdraw to their own people" and that sometimes they attend churches only "to get material needs met."[24] Her colleague Sister Marlosh fears that the Vietnamese are misunderstanding the meaning of religion in their lives:

> A lot of them [Vietnamese] say that they're Catholic, because they came through our agency [Roman Catholic Social Services Agency], but not really. Some of the refugees say they are strict Catholics, but when the Baptist minister offers them more food, they join the Baptist church.

In a lecture at the Indochinese Refugees Resettlement and Adjustment Conference sponsored by the Vietnamese American Association of Oklahoma City in 1981, Dr. Vuong Gia Thuy of Temple University addressed the importance of religion to the Vietnamese. He also commented on some of the cross-cultural misunderstandings which had occurred as a result of miscommunication concerning converting to a church or religion. Many times the sponsoring agency or person questioned the Vietnamese about interest in being converted, and the positive response by the refugee—designed to show appreciation, not declare a change of religion—was understood by the questioner as a response of faith.

> In order to understand the Indochinese, one has to understand his religion. In order to understand the Vietnamese one also has to understand their religion. The Vietnamese are open to Christianity for reasons of survival. They are not open to Christian religious beliefs. They normally do not adopt Christian moral values, and instead retain their own. Even if they go to a church, they keep the values of Vietnamese religions.[25]

How widespread these misconceptions may be is difficult to gauge. To be sure, Father Bao of the Cathedral of Our Lady of Perpetual Help in Oklahoma City believes that most Vietnamese Roman Catholics are genuine in their religion:

> Catholics have kept their faith alive and are growing good. Some have gone to other churches [Protestant] but most are faithful. They come to worship and there are masses in Vietnamese and English. As Vietnamese-Catholics we are thankful to [the] U.S. people for their help. They helped me here [in the church] with my English. (Laughing) I speak English like an Okie.

For the Vietnamese, their religion plays a primary role both in personal and community self-identity, and in the resettlement process. In Southern California, a Cao Dai group claims to have spiritual conversations with ancestors who advise them on how to adjust properly in America. Vietnamese Buddhists in Oklahoma have sung the national anthem of South Vietnam before mass on a Sunday morning, and refugees in Kansas who practice Confucian ethics have remarked that it is the chain back to their beginnings.[26]

Religion also serves the Vietnamese psychologically. It is the bridge the Vietnamese use to walk back and forth between the two cultures. Religion, assimilative and syncretistic, provides an opportunity to be absorbed into a new society without losing one's identity. It is a haven into which one can retreat when the "new world" becomes too confusing. It is the pole that provides balance while the Vietnamese refugees walk the tightrope between being Vietnamese and being American.

Vietnamese Community Organizations

Within the growing Vietnamese communities across America there have developed a large and varied number of community organizations. These range in scope from language schools to community centers, from religious organizations to sponsoring groups. Most, if not all, have language classes and history courses for all ages and celebrate non-Buddhist traditional Vietnamese holidays including the anniversaries of the Hung Vuong Kings and the Trung Sisters and the annual celebration of Têt, the Vietnamese New Year.

The community centers are evolving into institutional pillars within the refugee communities. As the sponsoring programs become fatigued or as refugees break away from sponsors by choice, community centers are filling the void with both publicly funded and privately volunteered services. One program which illustrates the organizational strength of these centers is the Multicultural Community Center at 1314 N. Munger in Dallas, Texas.[27]

The Multicultural Community Center (MCC) was established in 1986 for the purpose of helping refugees become self-sufficient and adjust more fully to life in the United States. It is housed in a building with four other independent and individually funded agencies. MCC is funded through the Texas Department of Human Services with additional aid from the Catholic Charities job placement service, El Centro's English as a Second Language Program, and the Model Outreach for Refugee Employment. It is funded by non-Vietnamese agencies but employs as many Vietnamese as possible in order to make the center a "self-help" program: refugees helping refugees. Thu Suong Tran, the Information and Referral Specialist of the MCC, is only one of several Vietnamese on staff, and refugees from other countries are also represented, since the MCC also assists European and Central American refugees.[28]

The center provides five basic services, and these are typical of dozens of centers throughout major urban complexes. Information and referral services are available with someone to assist the refugee in any of the three Vietnamese dialects. Caseworkers are on call to help with social needs, family problems, substance abuse cases, educational referrals, and financial problems. Legal needs are met as one of the five basic services due to the special needs of refugees for advice on immigration difficulties, labor issues, matters of divorce, and justice in the marketplace. Youth services including a youth summer employment bureau have been established and senior citizens' programs are also coordinated through the center. Nguyen Ro, Coordinator of the Vietnamese Elderly Association of Dallas, works out of the MCC to provide activities for senior Vietnamese refugees and hopes one day that the VEAD can construct and staff a housing complex for its members.[29] In the meantime Mr. Nguyen, along with volunteers who donate their time to tutor and help in other ways, coordinate their efforts through the center which houses the MCC.

Not all centers are as broadly based as the Multicultural Community Center of Dallas. As extended families located one another and moved into the same vicinity with relatives, and as the sheer numbers of Vietnamese increased, some of the community organizations narrowed their memberships to political orientations, religious preference, or economic standing. As this happened, centers became competitive, fragmenting the community rather than uniting it. The creation of support groups, which has been a hallmark of the centers, became less important than becoming a member of the "right" center and associating with the proper leadership. Fortunately, most of the centers continue to remain "politically free" and the services they provide help to cohesively bond the refugees together while advancing their adaptation within their host society.

Mutual Assistance Associations

Mutual Assistance Associations, most of which were formed in 1975 or shortly thereafter, are private, nonprofit organizations which, unlike many organizations in refugee communities, are managed and operated by refugees. They are unusually successful, since refugees prefer first seeking assistance from other refugees when those refugees have the resources and resourcefulness to aid them.

The MAAs across the country are linked together as a network of associations, although in the local community they exercise autonomy. Generally speaking, the MAAs promote mutual understanding and friendship between Vietnamese and Americans; assist refugees in securing places of employment; provide classes in beginning, intermediate, and advanced English; provide tutors for societal skills such as learning to drive a car; serve as a clearing house for community news; and encourage the preservation of the Vietnamese culture within the United States. Counseling services are usually free or based on the ability to pay, and family reunification assistance is provided through the MAA network.

As the MAAs become more established they are also becoming more politically powerful. They now lobby their congressional representatives concerning refugee issues and matters germane to Southeast Asia. They have formed some potentially powerful political action and advocacy groups, and raise money to support selected political candidates or help Vietnamese refugees escape Vietnam. They organize conferences to address refugee issues and to keep the plight of Southeast Asian refugees before the American people.

The problems faced by most Mutual Assistance Associations are twofold: donor fatigue and fund raising. Donor fatigue includes the inability of MAAs to find volunteers who can or will donate their time to work within the various programs.[30] Since most of the programs are predicated on unpaid volunteers this is a problem of serious magnitude especially as fund raising efforts prove less fruitful.

Mutual Assistance Associations have a particular difficulty in raising money for their programs. The clientele who has benefited from the center's services and who traditionally would then turn around and become contributors, generally have little or nothing to give. Those who are able to contribute have often expressed the idea that it is the responsibility of the U.S. government to financially support social services including the MAAs. Funding programs, then, have required government grants and corporate support in order to survive. Discovering ways of tapping into their own ethnic populations continues to be a source of study for MAA leaders and also a source of frustration.

IV

THE VIETNAMESE-AMERICAN COMMUNITY

Adaptation and Stabilization

One of the foremost strengths affecting Vietnamese refugee adaptation and adjustment to the United States has been the formation of communities. Vietnamese communities in America are proving to be strong pillars for assisting refugees in their adjustment economically, spiritually, psychologically, and symbolically. Their communities are supportive through continuing many of the traditional practices of Vietnam, while simultaneously encouraging changes necessary to adapt successfully.

The desire to change is a prerequisite for adjustment into another culture and the Vietnamese communities are programatically integrating the old and the new. Everyday events focus on the need to understand the new society, and to change at least in degree if not in kind. The community provides a workshop where refugees can experiment with the new but quickly return to the old for their security and in some sense control the rate of change. Such a meshing of Vietnamese and American values and practices is seen in New Orleans, Oklahoma City, Dallas, Kansas City, and Southern California.

> I feel Vietnamese, most definitely, but I don't like to choose between Vietnamese and American. I happen to go to Vietnamese cultural activities, and I happen to go to American

cultural activities. It's just normal to do both. I don't want to
make any barriers between them. [Vi Le, seventeen years old,
Oklahoma City][1]

Adjusting at a rate which does not disrupt one's personal
and social equilibrium is a difficult task for an individual to
achieve, much less for an entire community. One reason is
that even simple matters can become disturbing and complex
and the usual can appear to be quite unusual. In Oklahoma
City, the Vietnamese-American Association has begun a
volunteer program where previously settled refugees escort
new arrivals on their first shopping experience in an American grocery store. This need was highlighted when a family
of refugees first visited a large Safeway store without any
previous instruction or explanation on what they might
encounter and became frightened. In Vietnam, jars and bot-
tles were either clear so one could see the contents, or had a
label with a picture of the plant or source of the product.
Creative packaging was not the norm, and when the newly
arrived family saw Frankenberries cereal and Little Debbie
snack cakes they did not know what to think. Assuming that
the picture on the package literally showed what the contents
would be, the mother was horrified at jars of Gerber's baby
food with a picture of a small child on the front. Misunderstanding the message, she worried that Americans practiced
cannibalism.[2] With their recent experiences, the family was a
bit unstable to begin with, and this unfortunate experience
did nothing to help them adjust to a foreign society.

Realizing the unnecessary trauma caused by this incident,
the Vietnamese-American Association began a systematic
program of assistance to new refugees. Its counseling programs now deal with such mundane matters such as how to
read a contract, how to buy a car, and how to shop. Basics
which are often taken for granted are discussed. People are
taught how to make change, how to identify basic fruits and
vegetables, and what a medical prescription means. The goal
of the VAA is to provide as much stability for the refugee as
possible, not only in a geographical transition, but also in the
cultural transition which touches every area of their lives.

Cultural Continuity

Previous studies on Japanese-American and Chinese-American communities in the United States have generally agreed that assimilation has been more greatly desired by Japanese-Americans and less so by Chinese-Americans. Stanford Lyman in *The Asian in North America* (1970) states that Walter Beach in his article "Some Considerations in Regard to Race Segregation in California"[3] reaches the conclusion that Japanese immigrants tended to adopt Western ways more readily than Chinese immigrants who were more apt to congregate in segregated communities. Vietnamese-Americans have themselves began to show evolving community patterns which contain elements of both the Japanese-American and Chinese-American acculturation processes. The distinctiveness of the Vietnamese communities, however, is found in their resistance to change, their degree of resilience and adaptability, and a retention of old world values. At the same time that the Vietnamese are adjusting to the United States, they are working to maintain a strong element of cultural continuity from Southeast Asia.[4]

One of the ways in which cultural continuity is achieved in a new society and among a host culture is through a passive resistance to change. The Vietnamese are an independent people with an intense degree of ethnic identity. Although the Chinese ruled most of what is present-day Vietnam from 111 B.C. to A.D. 939, the Vietnamese did not lose their cultural identity. They rejected Chinese social institutions and national customs, and refused to culturally capitulate. In the United States, Le Xuan Khoa suggests that resistance is seen in the Vietnamese "tendency to cluster together and to form community organizations as sources of security."[5] These communities reinforce the tendency to prefer Vietnamese cultural practices over American cultural behavior.

The maintenance of traditional social units within the American society resembles the Chinese pattern of ethnically exclusive communities, but Vietnamese refugee communities are not as isolated as many of the Chinese-American neighborhoods. The passive resistance is an attempt to preserve an inheritance which many Vietnamese feel is slipping rapidly away from them and especially from their young people.

> The young people today are not growing up Vietnamese. They are too American. They cannot speak Vietnamese, they do not like our family ways of doing things. They like fast cars and fast food. In a few more years they will not be Vietnamese, or Vietnamese-American. They will just be Americans. [Mr. Thu, VAA, Oklahoma City]

As adolescents integrate themselves into American-style peer groups, they are becoming less interested in old country values and customs. Many teenagers believe that Vietnam is the country of their parents, but not their country at all.

> I came to this country when I was four and I do not remember anything about Vietnam. I have grown up an American and I am an American. I am not ashamed to be Vietnamese, that is not it. It is just that I have spent my life here and this is my country. . . . If I could go to Vietnam tomorrow to live, I would not go. It is my father's home and my grandfather's home and I respect them; but it is not my home. Oklahoma is my home; and I am an American. [Vietnamese teenager, fifteen years old, Oklahoma City]

The adaptability of Vietnamese people generally, and Vietnamese refugees specifically, has been a thread woven throughout their history and recent experience. Vietnamese are shrewd in their ability to use cultural elements—both ancient ones and ones acquired through cultural contact—as a catalyst to success. Their resiliency is due at least in part to cultural ingenuity which views macro-American society as neither a constituent nor an opponent, but rather as a necessary ingredient for survival. Understanding, employing, and appreciating American ways is a must from the Vietnamese perspective; adopting them is another consideration altogether.

It is at this point that most Vietnamese communities, and certainly most Vietnamese families, work to retain Southeast Asian values and cultural norms. The appreciation of new ways is encouraged, but syncretism mandates an integration of new and old systems, not a discarding of old ways.[6] Within the home, the Vietnamese language is spoken and traditional family respect and hierarchies are prominent. Folk tales from Vietnam, as well as other parts of mainland Southeast Asia, are exchanged around the family dinner table, and current events from the region are discussed. There is a concerted effort to teach children about Vietnam and their heritage.

This pattern is directly related to the Vietnamese status as refugees rather than immigrants. They continue to mourn the loss of their homeland, which they were forced to leave and from which they fled in a hurried fashion. They seek cultural continuity not in an attempt to deny the greatness of America, but rather as a strategy in adapting to selected patterns of the American culture for economic survival, while simultaneously honoring through local practice traditional values and belief systems underscoring an intense and proud ethnic identity.

The Boat People

Refugees from Vietnam commonly referred to as boat people include persons who left the country as part of the second wave of Indochinese refugees, as well as people who continue to leave the country today. Due to the broadness with which the term is used, it is difficult to define a boat person. In 1976, the United Nations High Commission for Refugees sought the cooperation of Western European nations, Canada, and Australia in accepting what were termed "boat cases": those persons escaping Vietnam who had been rejected by ports or countries close to Indochina and who did not have a place to go. "Boat cases" and "boat people" became synonymous in the literature and in the pleas by the UNHCR for refugee assistance.[7]

In order to accommodate the influx of boat people, the United States Immigration Service began to admit refugees in March 1977, under seventh preference visas.[8] Visas designated as seventh preference are those which apply to people escaping communism, or, if from the Middle East, fleeing

religious, racial, or political persecution. A seventh preference visa allows a person to enter the United States for the
temporary period of two years. After the initial period, the
refugee may seek immigrant status and eventually permanent residence in the United States.

Among those defined as boat people were a large percentage of ethnic Chinese. In 1979, when camps throughout the
Southeast Asian region were handling more than 50,000 arrivals a month, fifty to eighty percent of the arrivals were
ethnic Chinese fleeing Vietnam.[9] Since they were considered
political refugees, the ethnic Chinese were generally granted
asylum and their status was not closely scrutinized under
international law. As their numbers increased, however, the
legitimacy of their status came into question and host countries began to change their perspective and look upon them as
economic refugees. As a result, almost all boat people came
under new examination, and by 1981 host countries were
seeking ways to curb the entry of new arrivals.

This rejection by the host countries was not based purely
on assistance fatigue. Following the fall of Saigon, the Vietnamese government began a strategy of reconstruction which
involved reeducation camps, new economic zones, and the
nationalization of private enterprise. The reeducation camps
were subtly disguised places of indoctrination and torture.
Any refugee fleeing these camps was certainly understood to
be a political refugee. The new economic zones, however,
redefined the economic goals for Vietnam and subsequently
undermined the ability of persons to economically sustain
themselves. For instance, in 1976, the Vietnamese government adopted a Five-Year Development Plan which involved
population relocation from urban to rural areas. The
rationale behind this mandatory shifting of the population
was that it would alleviate overcrowding in the cities, provide employment for workers from the cities, and enhance
agricultural production in new economic zones.[10] This policy
coupled with the nationalization of all major forms of production, distribution, and economic exchange, effectively
eliminated private ownership and entrepreneurship.

Many governments labeled those fleeing these draconian

policies as economic refugees. The ethnic Chinese, who had often been owners of private enterprises, controlled industry, or regulated commerce and trade, were some of the hardest hit. Choosing to flee rather than accept a reduced standard of living and a degenerating societal status, the ethnic Chinese boat people were nevertheless seen as leaving a country where they were economically deprived but not politically persecuted. The boat people saw little difference in the definitional arguments, but were still the recipients of a label which made them unwelcome in host countries, and which placed them at a disadvantage even among other Vietnamese refugees. Seeking prosperity was not viewed as an adequate reason for flight.

The Orderly Departure Program

With the increasing numbers of people seeking asylum in Southeast Asia, an attempt to regulate the exodus from Vietnam was made both to control the flow of numbers and to instill some safe alternative to boat departures. On May 31, 1979, the United Nations High Commission for Refugees and the Socialist Republic of Vietnam created the Orderly Departure Program (ODP).[11] At the time of its inception, the UNHCR negotiated resettlement arrangements with more than twenty countries, including the United States. Vietnamese nationals who emigrated to the United States through the Orderly Departure Program were processed as refugees under the Refugee Act of 1980 or as holders of immigrant visas under the Immigration and Nationality Act.

Vietnamese nationals may qualify for entrance into the United States through the ODP under any one of three categories. Category 1 includes Vietnamese nationals who are close family members of persons in the United States. This is generally referred to as "family reunification" and according to the ODP "close family members" are defined as spouses, sons, daughters, parents, grandparents, and unmarried grandchildren. People in the United States who have close family members who are Vietnamese nationals living in Vietnam may apply to the program for those family members to emigrate to the United States.[12]

The second category includes former U.S. government employees with a minimum of one year's service to the American government after January 1, 1962, and individuals who were closely associated with the United States policies and programs in Vietnam. This made eligible persons who had former U.S. government employment in Indochina, employees of American businesses or organizations, and persons who had been directly hired by the U.S. for a variety of duties during the conflict. Category 2 also included former personnel of the Republic of Vietnam's government, members of South Vietnam's military services, and all persons who had allied themselves in any manner with the political and military goals of the United States in Vietnam.[13] Under this classification, spouses, dependent children, unmarried children, and others dependent on Orderly Departure Program candidates to the United States may apply to accompany the applicant for resettlement in America.

The third category includes persons with other close ties to the United States not fully defined by the first two categories. These included, but were not limited to, persons who had studied in the United States, people who studied outside Vietnam under the sponsorship of the U.S. government, persons who had held positions in the civil administration of South Vietnam, military personnel or others who had received American combat awards or decorations, and Vietnamese nationals who had suffered penalties or deprivation due to their association with the United States government or the American forces in Vietnam.[14]

One of the most visible groups housed within the third category is Amerasians. An Amerasian is defined, for the purposes of the ODP, as a person born in Vietnam following January 1962 and prior to January 1, 1976 and who was fathered by a citizen of the United States. Under this classification, Amerasians are not required to produce proof of American parentage. An interview is conducted by a consular officer of the ODP program who substantiates the applicant's Amerasian status through simple observation. If the person has the physical features of a Caucasian or Black American, he or she is generally accepted as being the offspring of an American-Vietnamese relationship.

Beyond these three categories it is difficult to gain appropriate classification for entrance into the United States. The U.S. government does on a limited basis consider cases of special humanitarian concern which do not correlate to any of the three categories,[15] but those cases are rare and highly involved politically and procedurally.

Once a person decides that they qualify for relocation through the ODP program a series of steps begins, initiated in Vietnam by the refugee or in the United States by a relative or friend. If a relative in America desires to bring family from Vietnam to the United States an Affidavit of Relationship (AOR) must be filed in addition to an application for family reunification. A friend or nonrelative may file an Immigrant Visa Petition (form 1-130) which is sent to the U.S. officials who conduct the ODP program from Bangkok. There the application is assigned a number, a case file is established, and assurances of financial support from the stateside supporter are verified. Altruistic persons interested in sponsoring families to whom they have no relationship and possibly do not even know may arrange to be a host family through one of many volunteer agencies. Usually the paperwork is coordinated in the U.S. by the volunteer or church agency who has already established a working relationship with governmental groups.

There are difficulties in the process, however, as evidenced by the action of the Vietnamese government in 1986. On January 1, 1986, the Socialist Republic of Vietnam unilaterally suspended interviews of applicants in the ODP program which were being held in Ho Chi Minh City. The UNHCR was restricted from processing Vietnamese nationals who wished to go to the U.S. or to any other host country. At issue was the right to determine who was actually a refugee qualified under the ODP program. Although the UNHCR, the Vietnamese government, and the U.S. had all agreed to the same general definitions, in practice the SRV and the U.S. were quite far apart. Vietnamese officials were submitting names of massive numbers of people who had not been pre-approved by the U.S. and simultaneously refusing to admit for interviews persons who had been identified by the U.S. as being of special importance to the American government. The net result was not a cessation of the program, but a sizable reduction in program entrants, interspersed with short disruptions as the debate ebbed and flowed.[16]

In September 1984, the initiatives of the Reagan administration were announced by George Schultz, the U.S. Secretary of State, concerning Amerasian children. For a period of three years the American government would admit all Amerasian children and family members into the U.S. In addition, prisoners held in reeducation camps would be admitted in abnormally large numbers with a target goal of 10,000 persons from 1984 to 1986. Formally proposing these initiatives to the UNHCR representatives and to the representatives of the Socialist Republic of Vietnam government in October 1984, in Geneva, Switzerland, the Reagan administration was encouraged by the Vietnamese response, which appeared favorable. The American perspective was tempered, however, by the Vietnamese government's interview suspensions and by bureaucratic red tape which followed. The ability of the U.S. government to expedite the process for the good of the Vietnamese nationals was effectively countered by their governmental counterparts.

In 1989, President Ronald Reagan authorized the resettlement of 94,000 refugees from all parts of the world for Fiscal Year 1989. Of this number, approximately 25,000 were to come from the Orderly Departure Program. The ODP was granted approval for admitting 12,000 Vietnamese and 13,000 Amerasians. Secretary Schultz stated that "An expanding ODP is vital as an alternative to boat departures and is a vital part of our strategy" [in Southeast Asia].[17]

Vietnamese boat people arriving at the Galang Processing Center, Indonesia, 1984. *Photo: United Nations/R. Burrows.*

Vietnamese refugees at the Pulau Bidong refugee camp in Malaysia, 1979. *Photo: United Nations/J. K. Isaac.*

The Pulau Bidong refugee camp, Malaysia, 1983. *Photo: United Nations/N. van Praag.*

Vietnamese refugees resting in the government dockyard area before being sent to refugee camps in Kowloon, Hong Kong, 1979. *Photo: United Nations/J. K. Isaac.*

Veterans from the ARVN Airborne Division participating in the U.S. Airborne's fiftieth anniversary parade, Washington, D.C., July 1990. *Photo:* Nguoi Viet Daily News (*Westminister, Calif.*).

Vietnamese Americans protesting Britain's forcible repatriation policies in front of the British Consulate, Los Angeles, January 1990. *Photo:* Nguoi Viet Daily News.

Vietnamese community elders performing rituals in front of the Altar of the Fatherland during the celebration of Têt, Southern California, January 1990. *Photo:* Nguoi Viet Daily News.

Students practicing Vietnamese martial arts (*Viet Vo Dao*), Little Saigon, 1990. *Photo:* Nguoi Viet Daily News.

Children in traditional Vietnamese dress celebrating Têt, Golden West College, January 1990. *Photo:* Nguoi Viet Daily News.

Performance by Vietnamese children during awards banquet of the Asia Society of Oklahoma City, 1989. *Photo: Quang Pham.*

Vietnamese teenagers in Western dress and hairstyles. Oklahoma City, 1985. *Photo: Paul Rutledge.*

Vietnamese butcher. Honolulu, 1985. *Photo: Deborah Booker.*

V

SOCIETAL INTEGRATION AND ADJUSTMENT

All over the world, there was a fascination with the plight of Vietnamese refugees and that of other Southeast Asians exiting Indochina following the fall of Saigon in 1975. Attention was focused on the human suffering and misery which followed the uniting of Vietnam under the Communist government from the North. Many Americans felt at least partially responsible for the refugees' plight and readily coordinated their efforts to assist in the genesis of relocation. Once resettling was in motion, however, Americans turned their attention back to other world events and to their everyday lives. The Vietnamese refugees, having newly arrived, began the process of establishing a new life in a relatively unknown country. For them, the rigors of societal integration and adjustment only began with entry into the United States and would prove to be a long and difficult journey. Pleased to be in America, the Vietnamese nevertheless now had to determine a way to become a part of the American mosaic and establish a life for their children with as near a return to normalcy as possible.

Employment

Upon entering the United States, many refugees began searching for employment. The need for income went beyond the simple necessity to place food on the family table. Survival was, of course, very important, and the need for food and other basics was a primary motive in the search for a job,

77

but in addition Vietnamese culture placed a strong emphasis on employment as an act of respectability. Unemployment resulted in a loss of face for adult males, as well as lowering the standard of living for the household. Finding employment in America was necessary for the maintenance of male self-esteem, for support of the family of origin, in order to generate income used for bribing officials in Vietnam who could then assist family members in their escape to America, and to generate additional monies which could be used to support the extended family and contribute to the relocation efforts of other newly arriving refugees.

Whereas some refugee or immigrant groups in America's past have been viewed as suspect in their desire to work and become self-sufficient, the Vietnamese refugees actively sought employment. The twofold procedure of seeking work and then accepting what work was available was modeled by the Vietnamese with the arrival of the first wave even though for most of the first and second wave arrivals this required a downward occupational mobility. Although some refugees found this downward economic move coupled with loss of status disorienting and often depressing, their willingness to pursue work and pay their own way is a mark of the resiliency of the Vietnamese refugees as a whole.

> In Vietnam, I was like your U.S. Senators. I was very respected and an important man, but when I came to your country I had to start all over again. I knew that I could not be in the government here so I asked my boys to help me think of ways that we could begin our own business here in Hawaii. It was after that when we started our lawn business and now I have nine crews working for me.
>
> I teach my boys that it is important to work for your living and that all hard work is honorable. I have changed from being a Vietnamese government official to being an American businessman. I am proud of what I do and of how my family has become Americans. [Vietnamese man, Kailua, Oahu, Hawaii]

For many refugees the search for a job meant accepting whatever was available. The initial goal was to find a job which provided enough income to feed one's family, and the secondary goal was to find the right kind of job. For persons who had held white collar jobs, finding employment which corresponded economically or sociologically to their position in Vietnam has been very difficult. White collar positions have traditionally been held in high esteem by Indochinese peoples while blue collar positions have been accorded little status.

In the search for employment, many refugees were surprised to learn that American businesses and institutions did not automatically recognize training or skills which they brought with them from Asia. Experience gained in Saigon did not necessarily translate into a job in Oklahoma City. Professional credentials were also carefully scrutinized by American employers and for many Vietnamese this was an insult.

> In Saigon, I was a surgeon and had practiced for many years. When I come here, I am told that I must be a beginner again and serve like an apprentice for two years. I have no choice so I will do it, but I have been wronged to be asked to do this. I am a good doctor and I do not have to be treated like a second-class [doctor]. [Vietnamese physician, Oklahoma]

Employment was found and accepted by refugees even when it contradicted skills previously learned. Between 1975 and 1977, fewer than 5 percent of heads of households were unemployed after twenty-seven months in Houston, Texas,[1] and in Oklahoma City, only 6 percent were unemployed during the same period.[2] The high employment rate among Vietnamese refugees was reflective of the strong work ethic among Vietnamese peoples. Translated into individual stories, this meant that persons who arrived in America often accepted work with which they had little identity, and for which they had no long term interest. For instance, Tho Van Tran was a pilot in the South Vietnamese Air Force and had no formal training other than his military background. When he first arrived he was given a job in a greenhouse in Little Rock, Arkansas, for two dollars an hour and within a year moved to Oklahoma where he worked as a welder's helper for minimum wage. He labored during the day and worked toward a college degree in the evening, graduating with a bachelor's degree in computer science. Presently, Tran works as a test set maintenance expert for AT&T in Oklahoma.[3]

In 1975 the early arrivals were generally assisted by acquaintances or friends whom they had known in Vietnam and who were American citizens. American sponsors were successful in securing entry level jobs for many Vietnamese, and the Vietnamese who were then employed developed strategies for assisting other refugees in finding employment. At the Fred Jones Ford dealership in Oklahoma City, one Vietnamese mechanic who spoke relatively fluent English was hired to work in the repair shop. After a few months of establishing his work record, he approached the management about hiring other refugees who had mechanical skills but who did not possess the necessary language ability. When he was asked how they could manage, he offered to serve as an interpreter and work at no extra pay as the group coordinator. The strategy was successful, and several other men were hired.

Finding a job was not always this easy; many obstacles stood in the way. Foremost among these hurdles was language acquisition. In order to be hired, change positions, advance in one's career, or even upgrade one's employment, communication in the mother tongue of the host country is normally required. In the United States where few Asian languages were spoken on a widespread basis, English became a lifeline for finding a job. Surveys conducted by the Office of Refugee Resettlement as well as local surveys by Vietnamese-American Associations have found that the employment rate among refugees who speak English with some degree of competency is approximately 51 percent, while the employment rate among those who do not is 6–9 percent depending on the geographical location.[4]

Another obstacle in maintaining and advancing in a job for many Vietnamese refugees is the indigenous concept of time. For the Vietnamese, time encompasses the past, the present, and the future and has an element of permanence. Time is perceived as having an integrity of its own and it cannot be hurried, rushed, or changed by humans. Consequently, the Vietnamese worker is not "clock-conscious" or "time-oriented" as are many Westerners. The attitude toward time is more relaxed than American attitudes and as long as one works hard the completion of the task is not important. The process is important; the fulfillment of the goal may require another lifetime.

Since the American mosaic of cultures places great emphasis on time, perceptual differences have sometimes resulted in cultural clashes. To Americans, "time is money," "time is fleeting," and "life is short." Underlying this philosophy is the belief that one has only one lifetime, and that it is necessary to quicken one's pace in order to accomplish as much as possible in that brief lifespan. Vietnamese refugees share with Americans a strong achievement orientation, but many do not believe that accomplishments are limited to a single lifetime. This different way of looking at time, unique in its variation from most Western perceptions, has sometimes resulted in negative analysis of the Vietnamese work ethic.

> Vietnamese are strange. They come to work when they feel like it, and they leave early. Sometimes they stay late, and sometimes they do not show up at all. If I can get them all here for several days in a row they will put out a lot of work, but I just can't count on them. I like the people just fine, but I just can't seem to figure them out. [Blue collar employer, Dallas, Texas]

Many Vietnamese have gone into business for themselves. Opening grocery and convenience stores, restaurants, clothing stores, jewelry and cultural outlets, tailor shops, beauty shops, and real estate offices, they found a built-in clientele among the refugee populations. Vietnamese plazas and mini-malls in Westminster, California; Oklahoma City, Oklahoma; Dallas, Houston, St. Louis, and Kansas City are becoming somewhat commonplace. Normally owned and operated by families, the establishments provide employment for both the nuclear family members and extended family members.

These family operated stores have begun to attract and hold patrons from the larger American communities. In St.

Louis the Jay International Food Store at 3172 South Grand Boulevard carries foods from Laos, Cambodia, Vietnam, Malaysia, India, Japan, Iran, Thailand, the Philippines, and several African countries. Persons from numerous ethnic groups shop at Jay's and it is a meeting place for those interested in ethnic cuisine. Refugees from Vietnam such as the Tran family grow Asian vegetables and have found an outlet for their enterprise at Jay's and other Asian stores in the L-shaped strip between South Grand and Chippewa streets.[5]

In Oklahoma, Hung So began with one small convenience store catering to Vietnamese people. Expanding to six stores in 1988, he now caters to the various tastes of Oklahomans and has named his chain "Friendly Food Convenience Stores" in order to include everyone.[6] Hung's stores are a few of the sixty-four Vietnamese-owned and operated stores in Oklahoma City, and are indicative of the growth of this refugee family industry in America, which includes continuing and changing patterns of business. For instance, Loc Van Le owns a Vietnamese restaurant which appeals to the American palate. Most of his food is more akin to Chinese-American cuisine than to traditional Vietnamese culture. In a conversation over lunch at his restuarant, Mr. Loc remarked that "my food is becoming Americanized. But that is good because most of my new customers are Americans who come back a lot."

Examples of Vietnamese refugees who have succeeded in the U.S. are growing exponentially by the year. There are, unfortunately, refugees who continue to have difficulty in finding work or in making an acceptable living. For the most part, however, the Vietnamese work ethic and sense of self-esteem related to hard work has facilitated refugees' search for jobs and self-reliance. In 1980, a study under the auspices of the Select Commission on Immigration and Refugee Policy showed that immigrants into the U.S. earned as much or more economically than the average American family within ten years of entry into the country. In addition, the survey found that immigrant families paid into the Treasury more in taxes than they used in welfare and social services.[7] Within just a few years following their admission, most refugee families are self-sufficient and contributors to American economic growth.

Occupational Characterizations and Patterns

The manner in which Vietnamese refugees adapt to the host culture is directly affected by their degree of cultural influence from Vietnam. Those who were born and lived for many years in Vietnam and were therefore enculturated to Vietnamese society respond quite differently from those who came to America as young children or who were born in the United States. Even the occupational characterizations and patterns reflect cultural influences brought from Southeast Asia.

In Vietnam the family took precedence over the individual. The group as defined in a variety of ways—family, extended kin, community—was always central and one's behavior was always placed in reference to the welfare of the whole. Patron-client relationships in which there were reciprocal albeit unequal exchanges between individuals and sometimes institutions were common.[8] In the United States, this sense of mutual responsibility has been easily translated into Vietnamese-American communities. The Mutual Assistance Associations act as patrons who provide or attempt to provide thorough job preparation, language instruction, and avenues to welfare benefits, the needs of the client—the newly arrived refugee—who in return provides loyalty and support for the organization. The system has been adapted from Vietnam, however, to involve persons who have been in the U.S. for a period of several years who take under their wing refugees who come with little or no preparation and little hope of survival without immediate assistance. Unlike the patron-client relationship in Indochina, the system within America has accentuated the interdependence of refugees and works on a more nearly equal basis. This is not to say that the leadership of the Vietnamese American Associations or the Mutual Assistance Associations equate themselves with new refugees, boat people, or in some cases ethnic Chinese refugees. It is to say that the system is diluted within this country, but nevertheless remains in place in most Vietnamese communities.

With the help of the MAA and/or local Vietnamese people, the attempt to find jobs for refugees is more than adequate but does not follow the normal patterns found in Indochina. Vietnamese have been willing in America to work multiple jobs and to accept night shifts. Some have worked in places which they would not have patronized in Vietnam, but find that it is mandatory as they get on their feet economically. Most women in Vietnam did not seek employment outside of the home, and the man was the principal provider for the household.

> I have a job at a little store [convenience store] where I work from 10 at night to 8 o'clock in the morning. I do not like to leave my family at night, but it is the only job I find. I am looking and I will find another job soon so I can work in the day. [Vietnamese man, Houston]

> It is hard for me to say that my wife makes more money than I [do]. She would not work if we were in Vietnam, but I have no choice here. [Vietnamese man, father of six New Orleans]

Many women sought work in the United States when they arrived unaccompanied by their husbands. Some of their spouses were in reeducation camps in Vietnam and would arrive later, some were widowed by the war or through the escape attempts, and some had been separated in flight and simply could not find one another for long periods of time. Interviews with refugee women indicate that they found work in privately owned shops, grew vegetables to sell to Vietnamese markets, and practiced home skills such as sewing in order to generate income. In 1984, families interviewed in Oklahoma City reported that 80 percent of the wives worked outside the home. Only 8 percent of the women within these families had no outside source of income.[9]

Occupations for the refugees evolved as they settled into specific communities. According to a study in Orange County,

California, occupations for refugees changed significantly from 1981 to 1984. In 1981, the top seven job categories were student, housewife, assembly line worker, electronics, machine operator, office worker, and technician. By 1984, the list had changed to electronics, assembly line worker, technician, office worker, machine operator, computer science industry, and self-employed.[10] These changes also reflect the reality that refugees like to work with other refugees. In Beaumont, Texas, the China Equipment Company, a local construction firm, hires only Vietnamese. The Tandy Corporation in Fort Worth has twenty-two refugee employees, and other companies such as Fred Jones Ford of Oklahoma City, A. A. Tool of Albuquerque, and Xuan-Thu Publishing of Los Alamos, California, have a dozen or more refugee employees.

The patterns of refugee employment are not purely self-motivated. The 1980 Refugee Act provides states with reimbursement for assistance to the Vietnamese refugees through the Refugee Cash Assistance Program (RCA) and the Refugee Medical Assistance Program (RMA) for thirty-six months following entry into the United States. In 1982, this provision was cut to a maximum of eighteen months, and Vietnamese are thereby encouraged to find a self-sustaining income as quickly as possible. This, too, then adds to the pressure for women to become employed and for many of the young people within the family to seek a job as well.

> When I came sixteen, I got a job at McDonald's to help my family. My father helped me find the job and I work part-time after school. When I get paid I give my paycheck to my father for the family. He gives me what I need and I am glad to do this. . . . One of my new friends, Adrian, told me I was stupid to do this. But I said that my dad gives me life and my family supports me. We all give ours [earnings] to the family and who needs it will have it. I don't think that I am stupid. [Pham, seventeen years old, Oklahoma]

The U.S. government has assisted in job training for Indochinese refugees. The primary focus of federal training policy has been to assist refugees in securing skills for short-term, low-skilled, entry-level jobs which would support them until they could enhance their education, learn English, and/ or find more appropriate employment. This would reduce the numbers of persons seeking public assistance and broaden the tax base. Generally speaking, however, the policy has failed. It has proved unsuccessful because the income from these jobs is grossly insufficient, because the jobs themselves were unstable and often eliminated, and because the cultural preferences of the Vietnamese—preferring to work in groups, work in ethnic businesses if possible, seek white collar employment where available, upgrade their educational level— ran counter to the government programs. The characteristics of Vietnamese employment mirror the philosophical foundations of their indigenous culture and as they adapt to the American economy they are finding ways to blend the two perspectives together.

Assistance Programs and Utilization

The federal government does not provide legal immigrants with any type of publicly financed assistance program for the first three years following their arrival. Immigrants are eligible for state funded programs which are prescribed for the general populace according to the laws of the particular state in which they are establishing residence, but federal money is not accessible regardless of the immigrant's level of income. Following the initial three year waiting period, legal immigrants to America become eligible for all social service programs along the same guidelines established for the U.S. population at large.[11]

Legalized aliens in the United States are ineligible for federally administered programs for the first five years of their legal residence in America and may or may not be eligible for state benefits according to the statutes of the individual states. Should the states decide to assist legalized aliens, federal programs are in place which reimburse the states for basic subsistence programs of food, medicine, and education.[12]

Unlike immigrants and legalized aliens, refugees qualify for federal assistance from the moment of their entry into the country. The Refugee Act of 1980 provides the legislative authority for constructing programs of special assistance to refugee people, and under current regulations the following services are available: reception and placement grants, cash assistance, medical assistance, social services, targeted assistance, transitional assistance to refugee children, health program for refugees, and English as a Second Language (ESL).

Placement grants are monies provided by the Bureau for Refugee Programs to voluntary agencies and private organizations which help in the resettling of refugees in their communities. The approved activities of volunteer agencies include pre-arrival identification of refugees, educational programs for sponsoring families, initial funding for housing assistance and relocation money, and orientation programs for arriving refugees. This may work in tandem with cash assistance programs which include Aid to Families with Dependent Children (AFDC), Supplemental Security Income Programs (SSI), and General Assistance Programs (GA) which are usually administered by state and local governments. The federal government under the cash assistance program will return to the states all refugee expenditures during the first two years of resettlement.

With some variation of eligibility, all refugees are given medical assistance for a minimum of one year and a maximum of two without cost to the refugee family. Social services such as employment counseling, health referral, translation, and English language assistance are provided by both states and the federal government. In addition, those areas of the country designated as "impact areas," geographical areas which have high concentrations of economically dependent refugees, qualify for federal funding under the "targeted assistance" program. The TA program is designed to assist overloaded states and municipalities while underwriting programs which enhance the obtainment of self-sufficiency. Other programs include funding to states for education for refugee children administered by the Department of Education; health programs through the Centers for Disease Control, which identifies specific refugee health problems; and English as a Second Language under the auspices of the Bureau for Refugee Programs.

The bulk of resettlement assistance is provided by the Office of Refugee Resettlement through a state administered program. A large portion of ORR's budget goes to states in the form of reimbursement for implementing the refugee resettlement program. In Fiscal Year 1984, over 78 percent of ORR's budget, approximately $425 million out of a $542 million budget, was passed to the states as reimbursements.[13]

The U.S. government, however, is not the only source for refugee resettlement funds. Small clubs which function as small lending institutions much like banks have been organized by established refugees for the benefit of non-established ones. Vietnamese associations, independent from and not to be confused with the Vietnamese-American Associations, make loans ranging from a few hundred dollars to as much as twenty thousand dollars, making it possible for refugee entrepreneurs to open businesses within ninety days or less of their arrival. Interest is paid on the loans to the associations, who then often increase the pool of money available to incoming families through a reinvestment of the profit.[14]

Economic assistance utilized by Vietnamese refugees is generally short-term. For instance, the use of government economic assistance programs in 1980 by Vietnamese in Oklahoma City reflects the rapidity of their successful adaptation to the United States. By 1980, only five years after initial entry, 72 percent of the Vietnamese community was receiving no monetary assistance from the American government. Of the remaining 28 percent, 5 percent utilized food stamps, 2 percent received money for higher education, 9 percent were utilizing medical assistance, and 9 percent were receiving direct cash assistance. Most Vietnamese preferred to be self-sufficient.

> I am thankful to the government for their help, but I do not need it [any more]. I think that a person should support their family as soon they can and not ask for outside help. My new

country has been good to me, and I want to show my apprecia-
tion by helping myself and helping others as soon as I can.
[Vietnamese deacon, Vietnamese Baptist Church, Oklahoma
City]

Coping and Education

To the Vietnamese, education has always been extremely
important. The educated have traditionally been held in high
esteem and given an honored place in the society.

A concept often mentioned by Vietnamese and one which is
considered a national characteristic is *"tran hieu hoc."* When
translated, the phrase means "love of learning," and the Vietnamese people consider it one of their primary attributes. It
is not the Western idea of intellectuals seeking eternal truth
in great libraries, but rather a traditional and deeply rooted
respect for education and for people of learning. The idea is
epitomized in the traditional Asian scholar with his beard
and long fingernails, sitting in the lotus position on a bamboo
mat studying the Confucian classics, but it is broader than
that.

The Vietnamese explain their love of learning with a story
of unknown origin about a farmer's wife who took a sheet of
rice paper away from her grandson after he had written on
the paper. She reverently burned the paper and the
calligraphic writing on it instead of allowing her grandson to
keep the paper and make a kite out of it, feeling that to use the
paper in such a frivolous way after it had been the carrier of
ideas and thoughts would be to desecrate it. Education and
entertainment have no equal footing.

Such ideas go back more than two thousand years.
Although most of the countries in peninsular Southeast Asia
were influenced by India, Vietnam was primarily influenced
by China and Chinese Confucianism. This historical tie largely shaped traditional Vietnamese educational systems and
cultural values and was introduced to Vietnam by a Chinese
mandarin, Tich Quang (Xi Guang) and later established as
the Confucianist examination system during the Tang dynas-
ty (618–906 B.C.).[15]

Following the independence of Vietnam in A.D. 939, the Chinese influence continued. The Vietnamese dynasties continued to predicate their governments on the Confucian model with influences from Buddhism, Taoism, and local religious traditions. Based on the Confucian system a scholar had four main goals or four periods of passage. These passages were (1) the perfection of his character, (2) the responsibility of family life, (3) assisting the king in administrative affairs, and (4) a responsibility to contribute to world peace and harmony. The major goal was to become a good man or a perfect man, a *"Quan tu."*[16] Should a person be able to attain only two or three of the goals he would become a teacher or a mandarin, both of which were held in the highest esteem. The system was directed at perfecting a person of goodwill, peace, and harmony with the universe.

Under the Chinese cultural influence, the Vietnamese dynasties and local governments did not finance the education of the people. Supervision was left to the teachers and private tutors, and the government chose to control only the competitive examinations which were necessary to enter government service. The language of instruction was Chinese and all materials were in the Chinese language, even though much had been translated into the Vietnamese romanized script. Under French colonial rule, the educational system changed considerably.[17] By 1918, the French had abolished the old Confucian system of examinations, and put in its place a system of Western learning. Beginning with the second grade, instruction was in French, and a basic Western philosophy was applied through a series of elementary schools, intermediate schools, and schools of higher education. Beginning in 1917, the French operated the University of Hanoi where classical lectures were presented by a staff composed of all French citizens, who inaugurated a curriculum which paralleled that of most French universities.

With the defeat of the French in 1954 and the advent of the first national Vietnamese government under Tran Trong Kim, education again underwent significant changes. The structural organization and much of the curriculum as developed by the French were maintained, but the medium of instruction became the Vietnamese language. Some curriculum was modified to meet the needs of a newly formed nation, and was adopted in dissimilar fashion in the two parts of Vietnam. In the North, education was modeled after the Marxist system which emphasized political indoctrination. In the South, the humanist model of the Western world was implemented with an interest in the development of the individual and the free society. In 1975, following the fall of Saigon, the northern Marxist model was superimposed on the southern region.

Following 1954, and prior to 1975, however, the southern region of Vietnam provided free education for all children. Education was revered, mandatory, but difficult to attain after the first five primary grades. Classes prepared students to advance beyond the elementary years while simultaneously teaching the basics to students who would not continue in the formalized process.[18] The classroom was teacher-oriented, and respect for the teacher as a symbol of learning and culture was foundational. The methodology of learning was memorization and repetition and children were taught not to question the teacher. Learning involved observation and listening, but not experimentation.

With this cultural heritage, the Vietnamese refugee children entered schools in America which were structured quite differently. Students are taught to question, investigate, and experiment. An inquisitive student is not considered disrespectful, but rather innovative. The teacher is not the source of all knowledge and may indeed be incorrect. Basic concepts are challenged in order that one may prove them more fully or eliminate them for a more nearly correct hypothesis. Time and tradition are not hallmarks of learning.

Given these cultural contradictions, the transition to American schools for refugee children has not been without travail. Bringing with them a tremendous respect for the teacher and a love of learning, they have been able to translate these values into catalysts for adaption to a new and "strange" system. Nevertheless, it continues to be difficult for some Vietnamese children to adjust to the American classroom.

I like my teacher, She is very nice, but I do not think that she likes me. When she asks me questions, I am quiet so she will know that I respect her. When I don't answer she thinks that I am not being kind. How can she think that of me? [Sixth grade girl, Oregon]

It took me a long time to learn that I am supposed to talk back [question] my teacher. My father got very angry with me for doing this, but I will not do well in school if I sit passively and do not ask questions.

Most of the time I act like an American at school but don't tell my father. At home I follow the Vietnamese customs. It makes it hard, but I am doing okay like that. [Eleventh grade boy, Dallas]

Education is important to the Vietnamese family and therefore gets a lot of attention at home. The focus of the family meal in the evening is often a discussion of the students' learning, grades, and homework. When the children arrive home they immediately begin to do their homework and if they do not have an adequate amount of homework, in the parents' opinion, sample problems or readings are provided. Saturday mornings are times for reviews, and special math classes or other classes of learning are generally the rule. Dr. Thuong Nguyen of Oklahoma City when interviewed by the *Sunday Oklahoman* (May 1) in 1988 told of his family practice of locking the television inside a plywood box so that the children would not be distracted from studying.[19] The telephone, television, and all other distractions were off limits during the study periods. Even so, Nguyen indicated that he was not satisfied with his daughter Thuy's graduation standing at her high school. With a 4.27 grade point on an accelerated 5 point standard and with recognition of her achievements by being honored as salutatorian of her graduating class at Northwest Classen High School, Thuy has excelled by all American standards. Her father's perspective is a bit different: "She should be better."[20]

Varying perspectives notwithstanding, Vietnamese refugee children are generally doing well in the American school system. Considering the fact that many spoke no English upon arrival their achievement levels are sometimes phenomenal. In a round table discussion with several refugee high school students they explained the reasons for their success as follows.

> I need to do well so that I can go to a really good university.
>
> I need to get a good job in order for me to take care of my parents someday.
>
> The only way to get ahead and to get respect is to make good grades. I make all A's, but so do a lot of students. That's why I also try to win with my science project. It helps me to be respected.
>
> The best way to learn the American culture is to do good in school. I want to be an American and this is the way. [Group of seven high school students, Oklahoma City, 1988]

For Vietnamese adults, education is also important, even though it is not as formalized. Vietnamese adults participate in English language classes held at local churches, the Vietnamese-American Association, and by local tutors or sponsors. Enrollments in community colleges are common for adult refugees and degrees are pursued in evening classes while work is performed during the day. Courses at the Vietnamese-American Centers also include survival skills since many Vietnamese are uneducated in urban customs and procedures. The centers provide classes in shopping, using public transportation, banking and counting money, paying bills, proper behavior in grocery stores, interpersonal communication in informal situations, and going to the doctor.

> When I came to America I did not speak any English and I did not understand. I could not read the signs, and I could not fill out the forms [welfare papers, registration, etc.] My friends in the community [Vietnamese] told me of the classes and I attend. They have helped me to make a good life here and last week I passed my first English test. One day before [too] long, I will take the test and be a citizen. [Vietnamese man, Southern California]

Across the board, then, Vietnamese refugees are availing themselves of educational opportunities. The path has not always been without difficulty or without prejudice. The stereotype of Asian Americans as math wizards has hurt some Vietnamese students who do not particularly excel in that field and who are then denigrated as abnormal or failures. Moreover, the labeling which narrows Asian Americans academically is not only incorrect but unfair for the many who pursue musical careers, write poetry and literature, and study the social sciences. In 1987, 25 percent of the student population of New York City's Juilliard School of Music were Asian or Asian-Americans.[21]

It is also erroneous to label Asian-Americans generally, and Vietnamese specifically, as smarter than American students. The *Time* article by David Brand, "The New Whiz Kids: Why Asian-Americans are doing so well, and what it costs them," reported that a study by sociologists Ruben G. Rumbaut and Kenji Ima of San Diego State University found that in overall grade point averages, Asian-American students in San Diego from almost every Asian-American ethnic group outscored their Caucasian counterparts.[22] The higher averages are interpreted by some groups to mean that Vietnamese students are brighter than Americans in the sciences and math. Studies, however, do not corroborate that, and the pattern of disciplined study on a daily basis has more to do with the outcome of grade point comparisons than does inheritance. Certainly it needs to be said that there are Vietnamese kids who are not excelling in school, and who in violation of their cultural mandates have accepted scholastic mediocrity.

> I do not like being thought of as a nerd. I do more than study, and I play on the soccer team and I am in the drama club. People need to understand that we [Vietnamese] do participate in extracurricular activities. We work hard, but we are not weird. We are just us. [Vietnamese high school senior, Beaumont, Texas]

Sometimes the high level of achievement and performance by Vietnamese activates resentment. Students have been the focus of harassment and have complained of racist remarks.

> I was called "fish breath" and it made me angry. I am not a
> "chink" or a "slant eye." I do not like being called names and I
> know that most of my friends at school do not like it either.
> [Vietnamese girl, ninth grade]

For the most part, however, the incidents are diminishing
according to a panel of Vietnamese elders in Oklahoma City
convened informally in 1987. The students are encouraged to
continue their highly disciplined study and to be at the head
of their classes. The overwhelming perception was voiced by
Nguyen Tran, who said, "If we keep on doing well, and we do
not push ourselves, people will come to see us and like us as
we are. We must do well to survive and make a future for our
grandchildren and their grandchildren."

Transportation

Adjustment to the United States and a new society has
included for many Vietnamese an adjustment to new forms
and methods of transportation. Many urban areas do not
have comprehensive mass transit systems, and those that do
require an orientation to the systems before they can be used
extensively. In order to maintain family lifestyles, conform to
American time standards, and socially interact at churches,
shops, temples, and cultural meetings, transportation must
be accessible and manageable. It is not possible for most
persons whether Vietnamese or not to depend on pedestrian
travel for the bulk of their travel within an urban setting.

The purchase of an automobile, which would provide a
source of independent travel, remains difficult for many refugees. The first and second wave of refugees have been able to
purchase cars at a much higher rate than subsequent waves,
and those without an automobile are dependent on public
transportation or on the cordiality of friends or relatives.
Some families pool their money and purchase a family car
which is available to all members based on a priority sched-
ule relating to jobs, grocery shopping, worship, and identifiable needs within the group.

Perhaps the most disadvantaged by the transportation adjustment are the senior citizens. Not only is ownership of a car usually financially prohibitive, but the use of public transportation is often confusing. Those who would like to drive sometimes believe that they are too old to learn new rules and prefer to rely on family members for assistance. When public transportation is the only option, some prefer to remain at home rather than venture out due to fears and/or misgivings concerning the city itself.

> If I took the wrong thing [bus] I could be lost and not get back. I am afraid of being lost in such a big place. [Vietnamese woman, Fort Worth]

> I have seen your television [news] and I know that it is dangerous [in the city]. There is a lot of crime and I am old. If I get a cab or a bus or I walk someone could hit me on the head. I am not strong any more and so I stay at home a lot. Mostly I go when my grandson can take me. [Vietnamese elder, Tulsa]

Housing

The policy of the U.S. government in relocating early arrivals into America was to disperse them throughout the continental United States. Within a few years, however, Vietnamese refugees began to gravitate to urban areas where larger numbers of their kinspeople could be found and where a greater sense of community could be built. Today, the Vietnamese are continuing this pattern and in cities like New Orleans where they were initially dispersed among the general population they have begun to cluster together in smaller communities augmented by people moving into the city from the rural areas.

Making the move to a growing community of persons like oneself has proved to be of great psychological assistance to the Vietnamese in their adjustment to American society. Having moved, however, the Vietnamese almost always mention the difficulty they face in securing adequate housing. In meetings in New Orleans, Houston, Oklahoma City, Denver, and

Southern California the issues pertaining to housing problems and problems of residence were discussed and analyzed by Vietnamese leaders, most of whom agreed on the principal difficulties involved.

In securing housing, Vietnamese families often prefer to live in groups or in extended families. Fire codes in many cities limit the number of residents in a dwelling, and landlords whether of apartments or of single-family houses, are reluctant to rent to large family groups. This often causes difficulty for the Vietnamese who may have a cultural responsibility to care for extended members and who are honor bound to shelter them.

> We had a hard time finding a house to live in. Because there were eleven of us nobody wanted to rent us a place. They showed us places which were big but we could not afford them. So we finally got us a two-house place [duplex] and moved in. When we have friends arrive from Vietnam, we are glad to let them stay until they can find a house for themselves. Sometimes we have as many as twenty people, but we are happy to have a place of our own. [Vietnamese father, San Antonio, Texas]

For many Vietnamese refugees, particularly those of subsequent waves beyond the first and second, low incomes preclude their purchasing a house and in some instances even renting one large enough for their entire family. It is difficult to qualify for a home loan when the family or the head of the household does not have a work history or credit history in the United States, even when all family members are employed.[23] As an interim measure, many refugees have found low income housing in public projects, but the rents in these projects are often tied to family income, rising as the income of the family or head of the household increases. In addition, the projects are sometimes feared by refugees as centers of crime and violence.

> I am only here until I can save enough money to move to a better place. The problems [crime] are so bad that I do not want to raise my daughter in this neighborhood. I hope to move soon. [Vietnamese parent, Dallas]

Refugee community leaders have begun to address these problems. In Dallas, the Vietnamese Association for Elders is planning to purchase land and build a high-rise for Vietnamese people where they can find reasonable rents and maintain a controlled environment. In Southern California, a group of Vietnamese businessmen offer loans at low interest rates in order to help refugees locate in neighborhoods of their choice. In Seattle, loans for businesses which provide housing on a second or multiple story are available to new or short-term arrivals.[24] A number of first and second wave refugees, who were generally the more affluent and who for the most part are residing in privately owned houses, have purchased additional property or apartment complexes, renovated them, and now rent them to other Vietnamese. The strong sense of community responsibility is leading the Vietnamese into a variety of innovative answers to the housing problems, as expressed by one of the Buddhist elders in Oklahoma City: "We take care of each other just like we did at home [in Vietnam]. If we do not take care of each other who will do it?"

Health Care and Cultural Values

Refugees entering the United States often have health problems due to the lack of medical services available in Vietnam and due to environmental conditions of their country. Immediately upon admission to refugee camps in Asia, physicians attempted to address the more pressing medical needs, but oftentimes, even in first asylum camps, the massive number of people and the overwhelming needs swamped the health care officials. Public health officials from the U.S. Center for Disease Control were sent to Southeast Asia to screen applicants who were seeking permanent resettlement in the United States, but again the workload was incomprehensible. It then became necessary, as persons slipped through the structural net, to station officers of the Public Health Service at American ports of entry in order to review medical records prior to final approval for entry. If unaddressed medical problems were discovered, PHS officials would notify state and local health representatives in the refugee settlement, and in extreme cases, the official could recommend quarantine.

The refugees from Vietnam who were in need of medical attention did not constitute a public health menace. Most suffered from problems due to neglect or unavailability of proper medicines, and treatments for most were relatively minor. Senior citizens from Vietnam brought with them ailments similar to those found in America's aging population: sensory loss, memory loss, arthritis, learning deficits, and other typical maladies.

More difficult in administering appropriate health services to Vietnamese refugees than their particular medical needs was an understanding of the manner in which Vietnamese view health and illness. An individual's approach to illness, disease, and wellness is culturally defined and is the result of enculturation or actual experience. The Vietnamese, who strongly identify with their traditional patterns of culture, continue to adhere to philosophies and practices whose origin can be traced back many generations while simultaneously employing an underlying sense of pragmatism concerning new methodologies. For that reason, they have tended to combine traditional methods with modern Western medical practices.[25] This accommodation toward health can best be understood in light of the way in which the refugees identify the cause of their illnesses. Traditional Southeast Asian health care recognizes three basic sources of ill health. These causes are physical, supernatural and metaphysical.

Physical causes are direct and apparent. A broken limb following a fall, an accidental cut while preparing a meal, or spoiled food resulting in an upset stomach are all physical or natural causes. Supernatural causes, however, are more complex and not necessarily so apparent. Ill health may be the result of demons, deities of various descriptions, or wandering souls who have returned to earth in anger. They may punish a person by causing an illness for an inappropriate behavior even though the person may not have intentionally offended anyone. The motives of the supernatural beings are not always clear and the offenses are not always recognizable although it is believed that some illnesses are directly associated with certain spirits. With this belief orientation, many Vietnamese seek healing not only for the physical symptoms of their problem, but for the supernatural cause as well.

The most commonly referred to supernatural cause remains "ill wind" or "bad wind." The Vietnamese call this phenomenon *Phong* and once it intrudes into the body it is the source of everything from hay fever to heart attacks. Traditional curing rituals have developed to deal with *Phong* and for many refugees these remain the only absolute cure.[26]

> I went to my American doctor and he gave me medicine for my cold. I tried to tell him that I needed something else, but he said that the medicine and drinking [fluids] was all I needed. I took the medicine for three days but I still worry about the *Phong*. [Finally] I call my friend who knows a Vietnamese healer and he came to my house and helped me. Only then was I getting better. [Vietnamese senior woman, Tulsa]

The metaphysical cause of illness can be traced back to Taoist concepts of balance. All living things including humans must seek to live in harmony with all other elements of life. Good health is the outcome of harmonious interaction; poor health is the result of disharmony. The two elements that must be in harmony for proper health are "hot" and "cold." These descriptive terms refer to energies and not to temperatures, and any disruption of their balance may result in maladies ranging from mild discomfort to mental instability.[27] Some ailments, such as diarrhea, are believed to be caused by an excess of "cold." Other health problems, such as pimples or skin irritations, are the result of a "hot" imbalance. Specifically, however, the imbalance partially negates the immune system and places the person at risk to almost any disease whether minor or serious. For Vietnamese refugees, recovery following an illness of almost any description involves the correct combination of hot and cold drugs, foods, and natural elements in order that the body may return to its proper balance.

Even with these perspectives, most Vietnamese, like many if not most Americans, would find it difficult to explain what they mean by "health." Given also the fact that with an introduction to Western medicine and a continuing orientation to American lifestyles, refugee perspectives toward health, as well as concepts of disease and wholeness, are evolving. Supernatural causes seem to be talked of with less confidence than five years ago, but it is difficult to measure if that is indeed a philosophical change or an adaptation to what is culturally acceptable.[28] The suspicion persists that perhaps it is more of a cultural compromise than a belief adjustment when mental health officials have noticed depression as a result of a refugee patient's inability to locate traditional curing practices or an Asian folk medicine practitioner.

> I think that American doctors are good but they do not have all [the remedies] they need.
> Uh huh, I go to a herbal doctor who has the right medicines for me. I take what the [American] doctor gives me but I also use the herbs. I think you should use it all. [Vietnamese man, Ft. Worth]

The cultural ignorance both of Vietnamese refugees concerning Western medicine and of American doctors concerning traditional Vietnamese practices can result in unfortunate miscommunication and on occasion gross misperceptions. In Oklahoma City, a family was reluctant to enter the hospital when they saw that the hospital rooms were painted white and the physicians and nurses wore white uniforms. To the Vietnamese family, white was symbolic of sorrow, death, and mourning. They interpreted the color symbols to mean that hospitals are places where you go to die, not places where you go to recover.[29]

On the other hand, American physicians responding in the manner by which they were schooled have misinterpreted their visible observations. Traditional healing rituals include *Cao Gio* (coin rubbing or coining) and *Tzowsa* (spooning).

These folk healing remedies have an honored place in many refugee communities and the Vietnamese are quite familiar with them. They involve rubbing the skin with a coin or the sides of a spoon to alleviate common symptoms of minor illnesses. This procedure normally produces bruising which has been diagnosed as child abuse by American doctors in Oklahoma City, Denver, and Seattle. The response by refugees has been not to curtail the practice, but to question the competency of the American doctor who has criticized the folk healing methodology.

> I do not know who is right. I know that my father used rubbing on me and his father used it on him. I will use it on my children because I love them, and I am angry when your doctors tell me I am hurting them. What do they know? Don't they know that Vietnamese love their children, too! [Vietnamese father, Westminster, California]

Mutual understanding on both sides is increasing rapidly as more studies are conducted in cross-cultural health patterns, and as groups such as the Transcultural Health Care Forum of the University of Hawaii John A. Burns School of Medicine publish manuals for health care professionals.[30]

There are, of course, some maladies which occur as a result of living in a new environment. Dietary problems have arisen from the fact that many Vietnamese have an intolerance to lactose, the sugar in milk products. Children beyond four or five years of age and most adults do not have the enzyme lactase necessary for properly digesting milk. Also, the change in diet may cause digestive problems. Refugees accustomed to rice, fish sauce, and vegetables have experienced cramps and other side effects when rapidly changing to a diet based on sugars, white breads, and carbonated beverages. "I cannot go to _____ [name of fast food restuarant]. My children like it but when I go in I can smell the grease and it makes me sick," says a Vietnamese father in Denver.

Health perspectives and cultural values can be learned. For the well being of refugee people and for the best communication between doctor and patient, dialogue should precede diagnosis.

Mental Health Problems

Problems relating to mental health and aspects of mental well-being are sometimes difficult to diagnose among refugee populations and are especially difficult to treat among Vietnamese refugees. It has long been noted that mental health problems among refugee peoples are generally delayed. While in transit and seeking relocation, psychological symptoms denoting mental health needs are minimal. Once the decisions of basic living have been made, however, the problems of social adjustment make apparent the mental health needs. These needs are often brought on by the psychological stress of the flight. Once "settled," the sense of loss and depression begins to take its effects. For many Vietnamese refugees the loss of family, decreased social status, culture shock, and profound sense of isolation do not become overwhelming until approximately six months after entrance into the United States.[31] It is generally within the initial period of six to twenty-four months that mental health needs surface and require attention in the refugee community.

The difficulty in dealing with mental health among Vietnamese refugees is profound. In Vietnam, mental health is essentially unknown and to the refugees it is a new concept.[32] If a person in Vietnam had a "mental health problem" it meant he or she was crazy and could not live in the general society any longer. Persons with "mental health" problems were often taken to warehouses and confined in isolation from society.

> You cannot talk about mental health. I know what you mean, but you will offend people [Vietnamese] if you use those words. In Vietnam, you are crazy if you have mental health [problems]. You can be depressed, or lonely, or afraid. That is okay, but you cannot have a mental health problem. Depression and mental health are not the same to Vietnamese. If you tell someone he has a mental health problem, he will think that you are telling him that he is crazy. You must not use those words. [Dr. Vu, Vietnamese physician]

In an attempt to address this problem, the Vietnamese-American Association of Oklahoma City hosted an "Indochinese Refugee Resettlement Seminar" on October 3, 1980.[33] Although the principal topic was mental health, the words were infrequently used. Instead discussions centered on (1) the depression generated by the knowledge that family members remained in Vietnam, (2) the anxiety resulting from the loss of societal status, (3) the homesickness of many of the refugees resulting from the sudden and relatively unplanned departure from Vietnam, and (4) the characteristics of Vietnamese culture which contributed to the positive and negative aspects of mental health. This was one of the first but certainly not one of the last conferences to address mental health needs among Vietnamese refugees. Already at this early date a consensus was developing.

Most physicians and mental health practitioners tend to agree that the younger the refugee at the time of entry into America, the easier the transition will be. This does not mean that the young children who arrive or those who are born shortly after their parents' arrival are free from adjustment problems. Often the problems they face stem from their seeming lack of "Vietnamese-ness" to their parents or to the older Vietnamese community members.

> I love my children, but I do not always like what they are doing. My children want to spend less time with us [the family] and more time with their friends. They are not interested in their country's [the speaker was referring to Vietnam as the country of his children, one of whom was two on arrival, and the other who was born within six months of arrival] history, and they do not speak Vietnamese. Not my son who is eleven or my daughter who is almost fourteen speak Vietnamese as good as you [referring to the interviewer]. They are too Americanized but I can't do anything about it.
>
> If they want to be like some Americans, that is all right, but not to be Vietnamese is not okay. They are too much like Americans and this distresses me. [Vietnamese father, Oklahoma City]

Even following conferences, interviews, and thousands of hours of study, professionals cannot always agree on the most pressing issues facing refugees in the realm of mental health. The adjustment problems for culturally displaced persons is so varied, and success depends on so many variables— economic strength, language ability, contacts in the U.S.— that to delineate a formula for treating refugee needs would be too rigid and unfeasible. In addition, as was the custom in Vietnam, if a person showed tendencies toward "mental health problems" (referred to in Vietnam as "acting crazy," with an emphasis on "acting"), the problems were handled within the immediate or extended family.[34] Seldom were the difficulties or knowledge of those difficulties allowed to extend beyond family bounds. Therefore, by the time persons seek professional help in their new Western homeland, it is unclear as to what difficulties they may have undergone prior to consultation, but some insight is clear. Basic problems of mental health include, but are not limited to, dealing with violent experiences during the trip to America, anxiety concerning resettlement, loneliness and isolation, loss of cultural values, loss of social status, the Americanization of one's children, and unrealistic expectations of life in the United States.

All of these may lead to what is viewed as the foremost mental health problem among Vietnamese refugees, the problem of depression. Prevalent in all Vietnamese-American communities, depression as a by-product of psychological stress has on extreme occasion resulted in child abuse, problems with alcohol, wife abuse, and suicide. In most cases, depressed persons do no harm to others, and tend to handle, or attempt to handle, the depression by themselves. Suffering in silence, crying alone, or talking with a friend are the primary forms of therapy for the refugee depressed. Counselors of Vietnamese ethnic origin at Vietnamese-American Centers or MAAs, are also helpful when the refugee refuses to see a Western physician for fear of being stereotyped as "crazy."

> I have bad dreams and wake up crying but I cannot tell anyone. I feel guilty that I lived when some of my family died,

but I just try to be quiet and go on. No one wants to hear me complain. That would not be good. [Vietnamese woman, Wichita, Kansas]

I talk with people [Vietnamese refugees] every day who are depressed. I try to get them help when I can because I am not a trained doctor. Sometimes the best I can do is just listen because they will not talk to anybody else. [Ethnic Vietnamese counselor, Dallas]

All refugees, of course, are not depressed, and large numbers of Vietnamese have made adjustments before. The challenge of adjustment and resettlement is well understood, and problems are countered when they are faced collectively by the family as opposed by any one member of the family or community. The age of the refugee, level of education, employable skills, and community solidarity are variables in the rapidity and strength of the refugee's adjustment and may, in fact, work together to preclude problems of depression. Assisting also in the positive mental adjustment to a new host culture is the National Refugee Mental Health Project which provided approximately $2.5 million for mental health assistance. Funding was channeled through the Office of Refugee Health, the Public Health Service, and the National Institute of Mental Health.[35]

Interethnic Competition

Problems which have complicated the mental health adjustments of the Vietnamese refugees include interethnic competition and clashes. Where there have been misunderstandings between or among ethnic groups, the Vietnamese are reluctant to call for police assistance due to difficulties they have had in Asia with security forces. In attempts to rectify disagreements with other groups, refugees often find that their language ability is not adequate to express their point of view and they become frustrated. On some occasions, they are simply the victims of perceptions over which they have little or no control.

In Oklahoma City, Vietnamese refugees were misidentified as the "enemy" from Vietnam. In a south Oklahoma City area of lower income whites, strong objections were made when Vietnamese refugees began to rent and purchase residences within the neighborhood. Interviews with persons in the area resulted in comments such as:

> I bought myself a gun today. I don't think those damn Communists should be allowed to come over here and just take over. [Caucasian woman, thirty-four years old]

> I don't like them people being in here. They have some strange beliefs and they can kill you with their feet. I don't let my kids play down there and I don't even walk down there after dark. Can't we do something about them? [Caucasian woman, mother of five, twenty-six years old]

> It ain't right. We need these housing for our people. [Black male, twenty-five years of age]

> I didn't go to Vietnam so these bastards could just come right over here and move in with me. [Caucasian male, refused to give age]

> I just don't like 'em. I don't know why, I just don't. I don't got to have a reason. [Black woman, forty-six years of age]

In Denver, a difficulty arose between a portion of the Vietnamese population and the Hispanic population. When the influx of refugees became too great for the city administration, they directed the Vietnamese into a housing project which had been designated for Hispanics. The project, Lincoln Park, was nearing completion in August 1979 when the refugees were housed there, presumably on a temporary basis. Unknown to most of the Vietnamese, the project had been a source of pride for an ethnic group who had historically questioned the city's treatment of their population. Viewing this treatment of the Vietnamese as preferential, resentment arose toward the new arrivals, and conflicts broke out. Young Hispanics vandalized the cars of the refugees, and destroyed portions of the project by breaking windows, damaging water mains, and slashing tires.[36]

> I lived in the apartments when some of the boys came and broke our windows. I was afraid that they would hurt me and I was also afraid that my husband might hurt someone because he was so angry. I did not want to see anyone hurt, and I did not want my husband to go to jail. [Vietnamese woman, Denver]

In an attempt to cool the ethnic unrest, meetings were held between leaders of the Vietnamese and the Hispanic people. The conversation continued for several days both formally and informally, but reconciliation could not be reached. In a desire to avoid conflict, the twenty Vietnamese families in Lincoln Park moved. Unfortunately, because of the misunderstandings, ethnic labels and stereotypes developed, and the possibility for future conflict was not abated.

Conflicts did occur in other parts of the nation, and bitterness developed due to misunderstandings which quickly accelerated out of control. In Seabrook, Texas, Vietnamese fishermen violated traditional fishing areas of long-term fishermen and laid traps in areas that were reserved for certain families. Although there were no laws against fishing in selected areas, the Seabrook fishermen had by consensus worked out a system to prevent the area from being overfished so as to protect the livelihood of all concerned. The refugees were not privy to these "unwritten laws" and angry exchanges between various boating parties became common. One afternoon, Texas fishermen, outraged that the Vietnamese had laid traps in close proximity to theirs, proceeded to destroy the fishing apparatus of the refugees. In response, the Vietnamese rammed the boats of the Texas fishermen, and violence ensued. In the hostilities, one Texan was killed and deep-seated animosities developed.[37]

The conflict over fishing rights began to polarize the community into "them" and "us." At the trial of the Vietnamese fisherman accused of murder, there were clear indications of this polarization. Following the acquittal of the refugee on the grounds of self-defense, the residents of Seabrook met, and the Vietnamese apologized publicly, hoping to diffuse the hostility. Informal meetings followed with the older Seabrook fishermen explaining to the new fishermen what they considered to be appropriate and inappropriate behavior. In the words of one long-term resident, there was hope for peaceful coexistence.

> I guess we should of done that a long time ago [discussed the "rules"]. Once we talked about it, them people were okay. I think if we can ever forget what happened it will work out. [Seabrook tavern owner]

Intraethnic Competition

Intraethnic competition, competition and conflict among varying groups of Vietnamese, within the United States has occurred at a faster rate and at a deeper level than interethnic conflict. Based on regional differences in Vietnam, socioeconomic discrimination, and religious biases, intraethnic disharmony is increasing even as interethnic misunderstandings are decreasing.

In Vietnam, it was generally held that the country which had historically been divided into three parts—Cochin China, Tonking China, and Middle Annam—had a divided population according to personalities. Persons from the northern part of Vietnam were viewed by Southerners as intellectually snobbish and condescending. Persons from Middle Annam, or the central region, were stigmatized as aloof, inscrutable, and traditional.[38] Southerners, on the other hand, were more flexible, more progressive in technological change, more "liberal" in their religious practices. To be sure, one could get an argument on these personality traits depending on the regional origin of the speaker, but the geographical stereotypes persist even in America.

Supplemental to these historical perceptions are newly forming perspectives on Vietnamese communities in America. In a conversation with a Vietnamese woman who lives in Honolulu and who was educated at Smith College she delineated the three categories which she thinks are developing in the United States.[39] From her vantage point, Vietnamese fall into one of three groups: (1) those from well educated upper-class families in Vietnam, (2) those who moved into the urban areas of Vietnam and assimilated, and (3) those who were, and remain even in America, part of the peasantry. The marker for the category into which one falls is generally patterns of speech. She remarked that you can always tell well-educated Vietnamese by the manner in which they speak and regardless of the extent to which those in category two have assimilated, they will never be of an equal footing with those in category one.[40]

Similar feelings of superiority have been expressed by adherents of competing faiths. Buddhism and Christianity, particularly in the form of Roman Catholicism, have been in conflict throughout the history of South Vietnam since 1954 and those feelings are brought by communicants into local refugee communities. In Dallas, the competition between socioeconomic groups of refugees is evident in the beautiful new Buddhist temple built by the first and second wave Vietnamese which stands in contrast to the temple used by boat people, a dilapidated two-car garage.

In Oklahoma City, the intraethnic disharmony was apparent in the problem experienced by the Buddhist temple on 17th Street. The city council had an ordinance which requires all houses of worship to provide one off-street parking space for every four members. The restriction was not unilaterally enforced and could not have been met by the traditional, large Prostestant churches within the city and it was therefore generally overlooked. When residents of the neighborhoods complained about the Vietnamese presence, local officials closed the Buddhist temple which met in a house purchased by the Buddhist Association and they were not allowed to worship until the requirements of the ordinance were fulfilled. Even after providing a minimal amount of parking on the front lawn and an adjacent vacant lot, the temple did not have the resources to meet the off-street parking demands and sought representation from the Vietnamese-American Association. When the Buddhist Association requested assistance, the Vietnamese-American Association claimed that they were powerless to help and suggested that the temple relocate. Heated words were exchanged, and feelings which had roots in the past began to surface.

> The VAA is not supportive, because it is run by Catholics. If we were Catholics, we would receive the help we need. They have never helped Buddhists even though we are the majority from Vietnam. [Vietnamese Buddhist elder]

> I don't know why they do not get some help from people like you [referring to the interviewer]. We really are not in a position to help. We would like to, you know, but there are too many Catholics who would oppose it and they are too powerful for me to try to change. I'm sure they will find some help somewhere. If they had a really big problem, I am sure we would help. [Elected Vietnamese official, Vietnamese-American Association]

> I didn't know they had a problem over there [at the temple]. I haven't heard much about it. [The interviewer then asked if the businessperson being interviewed could have possibly been unaware of what was happening regarding the zoning ordinance.] I guess I did know something about it, but it does not concern me. I am a Catholic and not a Buddhist and Buddhist matters are not for me to decide. [Vietnamese grocery owner]

After numerous phone conversations and intervention by Vietnamese community leaders who were fearful that the disagreement within the refugee community would give the Vietnamese a bad reputation in Oklahoma City, the Vietnamese-American Association did support the reopening of the temple. The support, however, remained passive, and the lack of support for the Buddhist temple by leading Vietnamese Roman Catholics remains a sore spot for many refugees today.

An even greater matter of concern for Vietnamese leaders is the growing violence within refugee communities by refugees themselves. In Southern California, robbery, extortion, and murder has been perpetrated in tightly knit Vietnamese communities on refugees who are the victims of other Vietnamese. In Garden Grove, police have identified six different Vietnamese gangs and have characterized the members as former military specialists in Vietnam.[41] In Houston, Vietnamese gang members have been accused of demanding protection money from local business people, and threats of violence have followed when merchants have been slow to comply.

The intimidation of Vietnamese refugees, many of whom are ignorant of the nation's laws and who are frightened of local police forces, and the desire to protect the community's reputation have made refugee victims reticent about reporting crimes and pressing charges against their ethnic counterparts. Nevertheless, ground has been gained in several communities where Vietnamese leaders have publicly criticized the gang members and began educating refugees on the laws of their new country. The refugee communities are beginning to band together to fight back. "People who steal and kill are not real Vietnamese. They have broken our trust and do not deserve to be protected by us [Vietnamese]," says Mr. Nguyen of Dallas.

In the short span of fifteen years, the Vietnamese refugee populations of America are beginning to establish themselves and shape a new identity. They have systematically attempted to integrate into existing societies, and adjust to their new homeland, while simultaneously retaining the elements of their heritage which they consider foundational in their self-identity as Vietnamese.

VI

PERSONAL ADJUSTMENTS AND SELF-IDENTITY

The strategy employed by Vietnamese communities across America is one of adaptation; adaptation which positively enhances their adjustment to their new homeland while maintaining their ethnic identity. To that end, American customs serve as bridges of practicality. They help the refugee to "fit in," and they provide information about the new society. American customs, however, are not automatically internalized. From the Vietnamese perspective, one may practice a given behavior as a form of integration into the community without accepting it as a part of one's own value system.

Language Acquisition

For all refugees, language ability in the host country is the key to success. In Vietnam, refugees lived in a linguistically diverse nation and first and second wave entrants normally spoke multiple languages. The three basic dialects of Vietnamese were generally understood by all Vietnamese, and because of the French presence, many Vietnamese also spoke fluent French. English was introduced into Vietnam at a relatively late date in the country's history, but Vietnamese in government positions and commerce learned it with great skill.

For those who entered the United States with a knowledge

of English, the road to financial stability was relatively short. For those who came without it, the road has proven to be a great deal more difficult due to the great contrast between the two languages. For instance, Vietnamese is a tonal language with six principal tones. The tonal quality of pronunciation is primary in the word's meaning. The meaning of the word *ma* varies considerably depending on the whether the speaker uses the level tone (*ma* = ghost), breathy rising tone (*ma* = check), breathy falling tone (*ma* = but), falling-rising tone (*ma* = tomb), creaky rising tone (*ma* = horse), or the low falling tone (*ma* = rice plant).[1] In English, tones are not a part of the language.

Factors further complicating language acquisition for the refugees include basic Vietnamese rules of grammar: verbs do not change forms, articles are not used, plural endings on nouns do not occur, there are no prefixes or suffixes, there are no infinitives, and no distinction is made among pronouns (whereas, in English, there are subjective, objective, and possessive pronouns). This makes it particularly difficult to understand English rules which pluralize mouse to mice, duck to ducks, and fish to fish (for multiple numbers of the same species of fish), but fish to fishes (to denote multiple species). Spelling also becomes complicated beyond pluralizing with rules that include, but are not limited to, "i" before "e" except after "c" or when sounded like "a" as in neighbor and weigh.

For these reasons, Vietnamese who study the language following arrival find themselves mimicking the teacher in many instances where comprehension has not been achieved. In an English language class for intermediate level speakers at the Vietnamese-American Association in Oklahoma City, Charles Muzny, Assistant Director of the Center, demonstrated this fact as he taught a group of second-year language students.[2]

> Muzny: Did you go to the grocery store today?
> Class: Did you go to the grocery store today?
> Muzny: Do not repeat after me, but answer the question.
> Class: Do not repeat after me, but answer the question.
> Muzny: No. I want you to tell me if you went to the grocery
>   store today. Did you go to the store?

> Class: No. I want you to tell me if you went to the grocery store today. Did you go to the store?

The ability to acquire the language rests on a number of variables: economic needs, age of the learner, formal education or desire for more education, and exposure to English prior to entrance. Among older Vietnamese, fifty years of age or older, the English language is very difficult to learn and use with confidence. These older refugees just beginning the process of acquiring the language often find it easier to rely on friends or family for translations.

For the young, the situation is different. School age refugee children learn the language with some rapidity, which seems to be a universal for children in any society. In America, however, they have the benefit of listening to English on rock and roll radio stations, on television sets, and reading it in a variety of adolescent magazines. In the classroom, the children concentrate on the language as a method of pleasing the teacher and a means of identifying with American youth. Says a sixth-grade girl in New Orleans, "I learn English because it helps me to make friends and because I am an American. If I don't speak English, I don't have friends."

In order to assist refugees in their acquisition of English, a variety of programs have been started by governmental agencies, Vietnamese-American Associations, and volunteer agencies. Some of these have been mentioned previously, but one of the more effective programs is the family literacy program geared specifically for language-minority families. In this program, family members contribute to one another's literacy by including reading and writing as an integral part of family life. Originally designed to assist parents in helping their children learn a language, for the Vietnamese the program has worked in many directions. In some households, the children read to and teach their parents or grandparents. In other households, they teach each other the vocabularies of their day: school work for the children, professional vocabulary for the adults who work outside the home, household words for the entire family. Using the family as a resource for learning has been particularly useful to Vietnamese refugee families who have a strong sense of family and family interaction.

Emphasizing this aspect of adjustment, most Vietnamese people have some command of English, but the spectrum is wide. For this reason, Vietnamese-American Associations continue to serve as a focal point of the refugee community for the language programs which they provide. Reading, speaking, and nonverbal communication are taught by ethnic instructors who have a sensitivity to the frustration of trying to learn English. It may be the most difficult aspect of adjustment for refugees; especially for those who arrive with no benefit of formal education, like the boat person who says: "When I got to America, I did not read my own language [Vietnamese] so good, but I was a farmer. In this place, I have to read for eat. That makes it hard for me but it makes me force [myself] to learn."

Family Customs and Kinship

The family is the basic institution established by the Vietnamese people to provide physical, emotional, and social stability for its members and to perpetuate societal norms and standards. The traditional family in Vietnam is patriarchal, patrilineal, and patrilocal, often composed of from two to four generations under one roof, although essentially classless. Vietnamese differentiate between the immediate family, or *nha*, and the extended family, or *ho*. The immediate family consists of the nuclear family in addition to the husband's parents and the sons' spouses and offspring. The extended family is the immediate family plus family members of the same name and relatives who are residing in close proximity.

The concept of "family" among Vietnamese is complex. Each member of the family has a designated kinship term, and members usually refer to one another by these terms; "son," "brother," "sister." Everyone is expected to work for the well being of the family, since the group takes precedent over the individual, and within this social unit is a precise division of labor determined primarily by age and sex.[3] Unlike the

Chinese household, however, the father as the head of the household does not command absolute control over the other family members. The father, who has ultimate responsibility, works more as an authority-leader through delegating responsibility, including others in the decision making process, and collectively sharing responsibility for the economic, moral, social, and spiritual development of the family. In Vietnam, the father often worked outside the home, the mother cared for the children and the household, grandparents assisted in the rearing of the children, and the children helped by working in the fields, gardens, or in some other way, depending on their age, school responsibilities, and gender.

The roles within the family have been traditionally well defined. The father is the head of the family unit, and is responsible for maintaining family traditions and leading in ancestor worship. The economic and spiritual decisions of the family falls mainly within the father's domain and he is always to be treated with great respect. The mother is also treated with great respect, but in Vietnam was enculturated to follow three basic directives: submit to her father while under his care, obey her husband following marriage, follow the authority of her eldest son if widowed. Known as the "three obediences," these teachings served as the foundation of society's perception of the ideal Vietnamese woman and mother, ideals which were embellished by a number of societal precepts.[4] Vietnamese traditionalists largely consider that a "proper" or "virtuous" woman would be one who was a good homemaker with adequate cooking skills, had an appearance of modesty coupled with feminine graces, was soft spoken, and was above reproach in her moral conduct.[5]

The mother, however, was not as docile as perhaps this societal portrait may suggest. In the home, she was considered the "home minister," or *noi tuong*, and was responsible for harmony among family members, managing the family budget, and coordinating the family schedules. She was in reality equal to the father, and major decisions, although under the domain of the father, were normally jointly made by both parents. Even if she were widowed and came under the "third obedience" to the eldest son, the son would not generally make any decisions of importance to the family without consulting his mother.

In the Vietnamese family, children have been considered as wealth. To be childless was viewed as a tragedy, and married couples were expected to bear offspring. When children entered the family, the parents took the responsiblity for training them very seriously. At an early age, children were taught the principles of filial piety and respect. The rules of social conduct for children included respect for all elders, obedience to older siblings in the absence of one's parents, and loyalty to one's parents. These principles did not end when the children grew to adulthood and began families of their own. Filial piety, respect, and duty to one's family included providing for one's parents in their twilight years. Following the death of the parents, the eldest son was duty bound to care for the ancestral tombs, and to maintain ancestral worship or reverence for the departed parent.

Relationships as defined by filial piety included standards for siblings. Age priority required that younger siblings respect and obey older siblings. The eldest brother was in authority if the parents were not available, and had responsibility for the younger siblings in their absence. This authority was expected to be exercized in an atmosphere of consensus where possible, and always with a compassionate hand. One mark of a virtuous family was harmony between and among siblings.

Since the family often constituted relatives beyond the nuclear family, rules of behavior were constructed for extended family members also. Aunts and uncles were treated as though they were one's own parents. Blood relatives, by whatever description, were to be treated with the greatest respect, and one's moral obligation to assist any member of the family was absolute. It was widely held that awards or reprimands received by any one member reflected on the family unit as a whole. In the broadest sense, all members were responsible for all other members.

These foundations of interpersonal communication gleaned from ethical systems rooted in Confucianism, Taoism, and

Buddhism were consistently underscored by the importance of the family as "place." The home was where most important events in the life of the individual took place. For instance, ancestral worship took place in the home, rendering the home the center for religious worship. The celebration of Têt, the Vietnamese New Year, took place in several locations but one of the primary sites was the home. The home served as a school for society where enculturation concerning appropriate behavior was taught; a judicial system, where disagreements were adjudicated; a hospital, where children were born and where illnesses were treated by medical doctors or local shamans; a form of social security, as aging parents were cared for; and a funeral home, where the deceased were prepared for burial and remembered following burial or cremation. One's personal identity, self-esteem, and well being were intricately tied to the family and its central place in the life of Vietnamese society was continuously underscored through everyday behavior.

Family Size and Characteristics

Numerous studies have detailed the importance of family to Asian-American groups, but the Vietnamese family in America is a relatively new phenomenon. Like most Asian-Americans, Vietnamese find their essential support group within the immediate and extended families, and from this base work toward self-sufficiency. As a refugee population this is especially important, since displaced persons do not have time to acquire contacts in their resettlement country prior to arrival. For many refugees, not only is family important, it may be all that they have when they first arrive.

In a census conducted by the Vietnamese-American Association of Oklahoma City in 1980, it was discovered that the household of Vietnamese peoples was constituted as follows: nuclear family, 57 percent; extended family, 12 percent; single person living alone, 13 percent; married family without children, 8 percent; married, residing with sibling's family, 2 percent; divorced with children, 2 percent; widowed with children, 1 percent; and 5 percent were designated as other.[6] This study on the family organization of households in Oklahoma suggested that the characteristics of refugee households in America were in a process of change from traditional Vietnam. In 1985, Gardner, Robey and Smith reporting in the *Population Bulletin*,[7] noted that the average size of Vietnamese households in the United States was 4.4 persons. In their survey they documented the following: 55 percent of the households were extended families; 38 percent were nuclear families; and 7 percent were a combination of family members and non-relatives living in the same house. According to their findings, the Vietnamese have the largest number of extended family households of any of the Asian-American groups including the Filipinos, Koreans, Asian Indians, Chinese, and Japanese. In 1979, Montero studied the distribution of Vietnamese by family, surveying 1,570 families.[8] In that study, he discovered that the Vietnamese families in the United States incorporated populations ranging from one to eighteen. Almost 80 percent of the families ranged in size from three to eleven persons. One-person families comprised 6.1 percent; two-person families, 8.7 percent; families of three to five, 33.9 percent; families of six to eight, 32.4 percent; families of nine to eleven, 12.5 percent; families to twelve to fourteen, 3.9 percent; families of fifteen to seventeen, 1.5 percent; and families of eighteen or more, 0.4 percent.

The size and characteristics of Vietnamese-American households reflect a young population. Gardner, Robey, and Smith reported that the median age of Vietnamese was 21.5, 20.6 for males and 22.7 for females. Of those surveyed, 56 percent were males, 44 percent females, and the expectation for population growth is extremely high due to the "large numbers of Vietnamese in or about to enter the prime childbearing ages of the twenties and early thirties."[9] They also determined that Vietnamese-Americans were the only group among Asian-Americans who had a significant number of families headed by women, 14.2 percent. Some of the women arrived in the U.S. as war widows, some were separated from their husbands in flight and have not located them following resettlement, and others have husbands in Vietnam who have as yet been unable to leave.

The composition and size of Vietnamese refugee families continue to change as the process of adaptation continues. With the birth of Vietnamese-American children who do not have the same ties to traditional Vietnamese culture as the parents, American customs are increasingly molding a new shape for Vietnamese families. Cross-ethnic marriages, single family households, and job mobility for students graduating from college are also having an effect on the shaping of the family and although family loyalty remains high, the structure of the family is evolving rapidly into a hybrid social unit bearing resemblance both to the traditional Vietnamese family and to the traditional American family.

The Emerging Family and Economics

The historical values of the Vietnamese family were not automatically discarded when the refugees arrived, and, to be sure, many of the traditional values remain strong in Vietnamese-American communities. These values, however, were and continue to be tested not only by the trauma of the trip to America, but also by the American economic system which tends to intrude into the sense of Vietnamese family unity. In Vietnam, all of the members worked alongside one another, or if the children were students they were dependent on their parents for their survival. In the U.S., many of the young people work, and are becoming economically independent. Initially, children who worked outside of the home in the U.S. gave their paychecks to their fathers who then distributed the money to whomever needed it. The American pattern, that of a worker retaining his or her income for his or her desires, runs counter to the practices of the Vietnamese family unit. The commonality of the family economic system as practiced in Southeast Asia is gradually giving way to the independence of American individualism.

> When I first got my job at McDonalds, I always give my money to my father. When my [American] friends found out,

they laughed. They thought that that was funny. Now I need my money for my car, and for my dating. I tried to tell my father that this is how we do it in America, but I don't think he understands. He still thinks we are in Vietnam. [Vietnamese male, seventeen years old, Oklahoma City]

Vietnamese parents are encouraging their children to adjust and adapt, but for many it is difficult to watch their children become Americans. Realizing that their children comprehend the new society perhaps better than they do, parents are acquiescing to new customs, but reluctantly so.

My grandson drives a car all of the time. He doesn't want to spend time with the family, only with his friends. I tell him that the family is important, and he agrees, but he is always gone. He is not Vietnamese like me. He is an American. [Mr. Thu, seventy-seven years old, Oklahoma City]

Where traditionally family members, including young people, would have to receive parental permission before making individual purchases, that, too, is changing. Young people who work want to have a greater voice in how the money they earn is spent. Inevitably, economic independence leads to greater freedoms and a breakdown of old-style patterns. For instance, Vietnamese parents do not automatically require that their unmarried children live with them until they marry. Young women are allowed to rent apartments with other single friends, and young men who find good jobs while going to school may stay in another state during the summer recess and continue their employment.

Changes in the family economics also bring about changes in the family roles, much of which will be discussed later. However, one of the affected groups are Vietnamese senior citizens. With the growing freedom of young people, the generation gap, at least as perceived by elder Vietnamese, is growing rapidly. Grandparents who need the psychological security of the family structure are feeling disenfranchised and insecure as the basic value of their society crumbles around them.

I do not know what is happening. I talk to my granddaughter but she does not listen. If I had treated my grandmother with disrespect, my parents would have beat me until I learned how to act. I am lonely, because I feel like my granddaughter has already left and has no time for me. I am told by friends at the church where I study English that this is how American children do. But I cannot accept this, it is too hard. If I do not have my family, who do I have? [Vietnamese grandmother, sixty-eight years of age]

Thus, when young people gain economic independence it may result in rewards for them but cause depression among ascending generations. Without the young to drive them to the markets, stores, and often interpret for them, many elderly Vietnamese have experienced loneliness, depression, and an extreme sense of loss. The generational split becomes even more visible in dress, hairstyles, bodily adornment, and choice of music, much of which senior citizens do not object to except as it tends to take the young away from the family. Without transportation, and without an affluent income, isolation in the city is exacerbated by the growing social distance between generations—a distance whose genesis is a result of newly discovered and accepted socioeconomic standards and practices by Vietnamese adolescents and young adults.

There is, however, at least one constant maintained from the traditional Vietnamese family. All family members, regardless of where they reside, are expected to assist each other in times of crisis. The changes in family patterns due to the socioeconomic environment of America have not altered the primary perspective of the Vietnamese family. Ultimately, loyalty to the group is more important than individual achievement or personal independence.

Changing Roles within the Family

The traditional Vietnamese family has faced tremendous change in gender roles, family expectations, generational perspectives, and family relationships since arriving in the United States. Families in flight are often separated from children or spouses, and in resettlement women have found themselves the head of a household, assuming responsibilities for which they may feel unqualified. The loss of economic security, social status, and self-esteem often creates depression, and the role reversals which may occur have placed stress on marriage relationships. Divorce, spouse abuse, and substance abuse have resulted in some cases, and the adjustment is proving to be very difficult for many Vietnamese refugee people.[10]

The role of men within the family has changed drastically from the Vietnamese male perspective. In Vietnam where men generally dominated social settings, they are now living in a country which stresses gender equality. It may be argued that women were, in fact, more equal than the model set forth by Vietnamese males, and the gap between ideal behavior and everyday, or real, behavior tends to show the strong position of Vietnamese women. In Vietnam, the woman controlled domestic life, and, as described above, played an immensely important role in the family's solidarity. Nevertheless, the discrepancies between theory and practice notwithstanding, the independent status of women in America and the apparently weakening position of men vis-à-vis women within the home have been threatening to some refugee men. In exile, they feel that they have lost control over their cultural roots by having fled their country of origin, and now, perhaps, they are losing control over their family.

> Everything has changed here. In Vietnam, I would slap my wife and children to discipline them, . . . to let them know that I love them. Here in the United States, if I slap my wife she may call the police and I could be arrested. Our discipline has come apart [unraveled], and I think I am not in charge of my family any more. [Vietnamese elder, 53 years of age, Oklahoma City]

In Vietnam, the man, as the head of the household, was traditionally the sole provider for his family. He was not expected to assist with housework or to prepare meals. In America, where the man often has a wife who works outside the home, he is no longer the exclusive provider and is now being asked to assume a greater responsibility in domestic tasks. The authority associated with his traditional role has diminished and Vietnamese men are slowly adjusting to these new expectations. "Sometimes I cook, uh huh," admits a Vietnamese father of seven who lives in New Orleans. "I do the vegetables, and I help with housework when my wife is too tired. This is hard for me, but it is okay." The perspective of this man's wife does not coincide entirely with his, but the adjustment process to changing roles is seen clearly in their varying statements:

> Most of the time, my husband sits in his big chair and relaxes when he comes home from work. He helps me with some of the housework and sometimes cooking, but he is not very good. This is hard for him. It is also hard for me. I try to show him that he is still the head of the family and that his helping does not change that. [Vietnamese mother of seven, New Orleans]

The role of women within the family has changed considerably in the transition to America. While retaining the roles of wife and mother, Vietnamese refugee women have encountered new opportunities in the United States. These opportunities to attend school, work outside the home, and establish an identity which includes some degree of independence from one's husband have been both a blessing and a burden. Employment outside of the primary household has resulted in a restructuring of the family. Family pressures to assume more traditional roles have created some conflict, and the insecurity of some refugee males has created tension as well.

Refugee women in the American workforce have learned that the pressures are not limited to adjustments at home. They face the same difficulties and problems as other working American women, including wage and advancement discrepancies, inequities in evaluation, inadequate childcare, and insufficient pay scales.[11] Balancing these new challenges in the social environment with the changes at home, refugee women are perhaps changing more dramatically than anyone else within the family setting, and not all refugee women view the changes with the same enthusiasm.

The new changes are good for me and for my family. I like helping pay the family expenses, and I think my husband is starting to accept this. My children like it, too, because we have more money for clothes and we are planning to buy a bigger house. [Refugee woman, Southern California]

I like to work because I get a chance to meet more Americans and to know the city better. If I stay at home all day, I would not have anything to do. My husband works all day, and my children are in college, so it is good for me to get out of the house. [Refugee woman, Tulsa]

I think that money independence is hurting us [Vietnamese families]. At work, women are meeting American men and some are in trouble [having affairs], even some who are married. This independence of the family is causing divorce which we did not have like this in Vietnam. I think that it is very bad. [Refugee woman, California]

I don't know if it is good or bad. I just think that this is how we do it in America. So we will all just learn to live this way and still keep our families strong. [Refugee woman, Oklahoma City]

Among the many changes within the family, the most unacceptable to the Vietnamese community at large is that of divorce. The idea of men helping with the housework often draws snickers in a group conversation, the idea of women working outside the home is grudgingly accepted as an economic reality, but the growing number of divorces in the refugee community continues to be a source of deep concern on the part of community leaders. In Vietnam, divorce was essentially unknown, and until 1959 when polygyny was outlawed by the Vietnamese government, a man was responsible for his wife or wives for the duration of their lives. In cases of incompatibility, it was considered far better to have a mistress, or abandon the family, than to divorce.[12] In the United States, where divorce is socially acceptable, and where economic independence is far more accessible for both genders than in Southeast Asia, divorces have been on the rise. Figures are difficult to acquire since divorce is highly stigmatized among Vietnamese communities and because it is considered dishonorable by refugees. Local conversations, however, in Oklahoma City, Dallas, New Orleans, Kansas City, and Westminster indicate that Vietnamese-American Associations and other Mutual Assistance Associations have now added full time counselors to their staffs who spend considerable time working with couples considering divorce. In 1984, counseling was provided for thirty-two couples in Oklahoma City by the Indochinese Refugee Crisis Center,[13] and in Dallas, local ministers counseled several dozen Vietnamese couples who were considering separation or divorce.

Refugee children and adolescents are also faced with changes in societal and family roles. Within American society they face the identical problems as other American youth—peer pressure, aspects of self-identity, drug and alcohol abuse—in addition to language problems and the sense of loss. Refugee young people who have entered the U.S. as young children often arrive without a parent, sibling, or extended kinsperson who was lost during the flight from Vietnam, over the sea route, or separated during the asylum-camp experience. Disorientation is common, and at a time when they need special guidance and attention, the children's parents may be as confused as the children.

Introduced into an American educational system which is new and whose expectations are initially foreign, most refugee youth work diligently to achieve success in the American system. This work ethic which aids their adaptability has proven, also, to be a two-edged sword. The more successful they are in school, the more American they are perceived to be by their parents, and although their parents are extremely proud, they are leery of the distance caused by their child's growing American identity.

> My son speaks English better [than me] and he does not speak Vietnamese good. Sometimes I have to get him for understanding [translating] and this I don't like. It makes him think he is better [than me]. [Vietnamese elder, Tết Celebration, Oklahoma]

Learning English at a more rapid pace than many of their parents, refugee children are placed in a Catch-22 position.

They must learn the language to survive, but in their success they, by default, are relied upon by parents in more difficult language situations. This reliance creates a role reversal from traditional Vietnamese society, and sometimes results in conflict within the family. Consternation of the child or adolescent grows as he or she continues the attempt to live between two cultures: the Vietnamese culture of the home; the American culture of society.

The acceptance of a new standard by adolescents inevitably decreases the ties to historical precedents. The traditional value of obeying one's parents is not completely discarded by Vietnamese-American youth, but it is shared with outside influences and authorities. Often these influences are in conflict.

> My father tells me that I cannot smoke, but all my friends smoke. When I try to explain, he threatens to beat me. I have already made some plans, and if he tries to hurt me, I will leave. He cannot make me be like him. My father is very important to me, but lately we do not get along very well. I wish there was some way he could accept me. I am an American. I am not a Vietnamese like he is. [Vietnamese youth, sixteen years of age, Oklahoma City]

Refugee young people, who like many other American youth are at risk from illegal substances, alcohol abuse, and gang membership, are nevertheless excelling as a group in their principal endeavor: education. Maintaining the long-held value placed on education, the responsibility of children, second only to filial respect, is to achieve excellence in school. High educational performance is expected of both males and females, and following the school day, children are required to study after arriving at home. In some homes, watching television is only allowed on the weekends, and study is expected even if the teacher has not made assignments. In those cases, the parent may write questions for the child, or they may read ahead and study what they did in school during that day. The ultimate goal is a college education and graduate studies depending on the career chosen by the child in order that the child may obtain "appropriate standing" in the community. That is not to indicate, however, that all Vietnamese youth excel in their scholastic pursuits. The myth of Asian-American superiority in the classroom may be countered by those refugee youths who are average academically and who lack motivation to continue past high school. The success factor for Asian-Americans is tied to their respect for education and their tandem hard work in achieving an education, not to genetic factors or any magical abilities.

In concert with other family members who are introduced to unfamiliar customs in the social environment, Vietnamese children and young people come in contact with new behaviors and perspectives throughout their educational careers. Their response to date has been mixed; some of the new customs they readily accept, some they participate in but do not particularly adopt, and some they reject outright. They have maintained a respect for the family as a whole, and for parental leadership. They have rejected forms of extreme independence which would mandate moving outside the home, or acting out toward parents, but they have created a middle ground. They are acquiring and employing independence while retaining family ties. They are fashioning a new model of the Vietnamese-American communities of the twenty-first century.

Courtship, Marriage, and Family Traditions

For centuries, Vietnamese society held a concept of fate premised upon the goodwill of Heaven. It was believed that fate in marriage, wealth, and position were predestined by a merciful, compassionate, and just Heaven.[14] The concept of the will of Heaven, or of the gods, is a blending of Confucian philosophy and Buddhist theology, a belief that this world's fate is predicated upon actions and behaviors in one's previous life. To the Vietnamese, however, one's own will and choices play a part in fate. One may choose to do well and therefore achieve a positive fate or choose to act in a malevolent fashion, thereby activating a negative fate.

This combination of control and destiny carries over into

refugee mentality regarding love and marriage. A person is free to think about love, mentally envision the one he or she would like to love, and hold thoughts of love for another person, but is not totally free to select the one whom he or she will marry. Thoughts of love are supposed to be secret, and the Western dating pattern is not practiced within traditional Vietnamese society.[15] Selecting one's marriage partner is the responsibility of the extended family, including parents, aunts, uncles, and grandparents. Filial piety requires that the young honor the wishes of their parents, and parents frequently arranged the marriages of their children. Over time, even in Vietnam, the practice of arranged marriages became somewhat diluted, as parents became more advisory than dictatorial and as young people were affected by Western customs and media.

Should a marriage be arranged by parents, the process was preordained. Having agreed, the two families engaged the services of a matchmaker who approached the families seeking official approval to announce the engagement of the couple. Once the engagement was made public, a waiting period of approximately six months was required prior to the marriage, and in the event of mourning, the wedding must be postponed until the period of mourning was concluded. The ceremony itself was normally held in the home, but in some instances, Roman Catholic and Buddhist weddings would begin in the church or the temple and conclude in the home. Celebrations of various lengths would follow, and the couple was then granted a certificate of marriage or simply pronounced married.

Many refugees fifty years of age and older speak of their arranged marriages. In most instances, however, the son had already spoken to his parents about his interest in a young woman whom he had met in a social situation, at school, or through community celebrations.[16] With the parents' concurrence, the usual matchmaking formalities were employed although the selection had been made by the couple themselves. Even so, dating prior to engagement was not allowed, and dating, as Americans practice it, was not common even during the engagement period.

In the U.S., patterns have changed as the families have become more settled. Interviews with refugee families across America indicate that the family continues to play a strong and in some cases a dominant role. The family continues to exercise input into the selection of a mate, although that assistance is not absolute. Vietnamese young people are involved in dating and go unchaperoned to dances, shows, and parties with members of the opposite sex. They develop interpersonally along the societal norms of American youth, and want to select the person with whom they will create a family. When that selection takes place, the family is involved by the youth, and in the event of a marriage proposal, the male's family approaches the female's family on behalf of the son to broach the idea of an engagement. The ceremonies are planned, and may take place at home, at a church or temple, or in a country club, hotel, or other secular gathering place.

From the parents' perspective, the most perplexing aspect of this process is dating. The American pattern of young men and women holding hands in public, embracing, or kissing is absolutely forbidden in Vietnam. Hand holding as an act of friendship was allowed, but only by two persons of the same sex, never by members of the opposite sex.[17] Virginity prior to marriage is highly valued, and the media attention given to premarital sex by young people in America is threatening to many parents.

> I do not allow my daughter to go out with a boy. She can go with a group of girls but not with a boy. There will be enough after marriage. I must be careful to watch her because she is not able to do [watch out] for herself. [Vietnamese mother of a seventeen-year-old daughter]
>
> I think that my son has dated, but he has not told me. He knows that I do not want him to date, but he is in the university [University of Oklahoma] and so he has a lot of his own time. I try to tell him to make good grades so he can get into medical school. I am afraid that if he has a lot of dating he will not have good grades. [Vietnamese father of a nineteen-year-old son]

With newly introduced patterns of dating, Vietnamese young people are also adopting material standards of dress, hair fashions, and bodily adornment. In Oklahoma City during the Têt festival, among those present was a group of young men who had spiked haircuts, loose-fitting trousers, brightly colored shirts with huge polka dots and other designs, and multiple earrings. Vietnamese adults standing in the corridors spoke openly about these young men.

> Disgusting. Why does his father let him do that? We should go and talk to him about this embarrassment. [Forty-eight-year-old male]

> I don't think the parents know. No one I know would let their kid dress like that. [Forty-four-year-old male]

> We are losing control. I cannot imagine what our young people will be like in ten years. [Fifty-three-year-old male]

> It's not as bad as it looks. I don't like it either, but they will grow out of it. I only worry that our daughters may want to do something like that, too. [Thirty-eight-year-old male]

Traditional practices from Southeast Asia are giving way to the more trendy fashions of American youth. The daughters of Vietnamese families are also dressing in the current styles, soliciting their parents to allow them to date, and on occasion dating without their parents' knowledge. Interracial and interethnic dating is becoming more common, and for many parents this is particularly difficult to accept. From the young person's point of view, they are only following the standards of the culture of which they are a part. Honoring their parents remains important to refugee youth; that does not exclude, however, participating in the American dating game and remaining free to date whomever they choose. Following a Têt celebration at a Vietnamese Buddhist Temple, one young man remarked, "My girlfriend is going to eat with my family for the first time tonight. I just hope the family likes her."

Amerasians and the Resettlement Process

Amerasians are unfortunately not new to the historical scene. Perhaps as early as the late 1800s during the Spanish-

American War, American troops in the Philippines fathered children by local women and then abandoned both mother and child. During the Vietnam conflict, undocumented numbers of children were fathered by American servicemen and then left behind when the father rotated home to the United States, or when his unit was relocated. Acknowledging responsibility for Amerasian children, Congressman Stuart McKinney introduced civil rights legislation in 1979 which would have provided care for children of American military parentage born after 1950 in Korea, Vietnam, Laos, and Thailand.[18] Although unsuccessful, it was the first in a series of attempts which finally resulted in the passage in 1982 of a bill accepting responsibility by the U.S. government for Amerasians as American citizens. This policy was challenged, however, by volunteer groups who claimed that the U.S. government did not adequately fund the necessary programs to bring Amerasians to the U.S. and that to date some of the legislation has only been cosmetic since owing to the lack of diplomatic relations between the two countries it did not cover Amerasians born in Vietnam. To counter these criticisms, and as an act of policy, the U.S. Department of State included Amerasians in the Orderly Departure Program. The intended net effect of this decision was to provide blanket coverage for persons of Amerasian identity who were not included in the original measure. Departure from Vietnam, however, continued at a relative snail's pace until the passage of the Amerasian Homecoming Act in December 1987. The Act established the desire of the United States to bring to America all Amerasians and family members by March 1990. Unrealistic in its time frame, the Act has been extended until September 1990, and will need further consideration following that deadline.

The exact number of Amerasian children has been debated and widely disputed. Numbers ranging from as small as 10,000 to more than 200,000 have been reported, and in 1989, *Refugee Reports* published a claim that there were approximately 30,000 Amerasian children.[20] The ethnicity of these children is also a matter of dispute and is open to debate. The best guesstimates, however, come from refugee workers in the field, associated with the American Red Cross and the United States Catholic Conference. Although no scientific figure exists, it is estimated that approximately 65 to 75 percent of the children are the offspring of Caucasian soldiers, and approximately 25 to 35 percent are the biological children of African-American soldiers. Those who are designated as black Amerasians encounter specific bias based on their racial heritage. To some Vietnamese, being black is a handicap[21] and a reason for scorn.

The number of Amerasians admitted to the United States is more easily documented than that of Amerasians in Vietnam and across Southeast Asia. In 1989, approximately 10,000 Amerasians and accompanying family members[22] were admitted to the U.S. and the ceiling admission figure has been raised for subsequent years. Of the almost one million Southeast Asian refugees in America, more than 22,000 are Amerasians,[23] and although they constitute only 2 to 3 percent of the refugee population, they nonetheless face particular problems in the resettlement process.

In an attempt to address these specific needs, Amerasians are generally routed to the United States through the Philippine Refugee Processing Center. In the camp they go through a six-month orientation period designed to help them adjust to the United States. The camp has proven, however, to be a point of congestion on the trip across the Pacific and it is questionable as to how much help the refugees receive while in residence. In addition, because the camp is so crowded, departures from Vietnam are slowed due to the inability of the camp to accept unlimited admissions.

Resettlement in the United States was also impeded by the lack of initial sponsorship. Since many Amerasians did not have relatives in America, or at least could not identify or locate stateside relations, resettlement could not begin until a sponsoring agency or individual had been coupled with the refugee. In locating sponsors for Amerasians, the U.S. government designated fifty locations throughout the country as "cluster sites" where Amerasians were resettled and where training could be provided to sponsors. Major prerequisites for selected cluster sites included experience in assisting refugees, adequate community social services, agencies sensitive to and trained in Amerasian needs analysis, and the availability of Vietnamese language interpreters.

One of the primary purposes of clustering Amerasians was to provide persons with whom they could identify and from whom they could find support. In order to establish their self-identity in a secondary host culture, Amerasians need encouragement from every source possible. Sometimes confused as to their own ethnic identity, they do not even fit the stereotypes of Vietnamese-Americans as held by many U.S. citizens.

> My father was white and my mother is Vietnamese. My father deserted me when I was young and I never met him, and my mother left sometime after that. I was raised by some of my mother's relatives, but I don't really know who my parents are. Because I am not really Vietnamese, I couldn't go to school in Vietnam, and I am behind in everything. Nobody really likes me. I don't really fit in to any group. [Amerasian male, twenty-four years of age; quote translated by author]

Amerasians have had a difficult time being accepted into the Vietnamese-American communities. If they have black heritage, the bias is often not subtle; if they have white heritage, it is more passive. A Vietnamese student at the University of Oklahoma says, "I don't like Amerasians. They don't do well in school and they are always in trouble. I am afraid that Americans will think that we are all like that."

Many Vietnamese people do not consider Amerasians as "legitimate" Vietnamese, and are upset at their lack of traditional Vietnamese cultural values even though many Amerasians are culturally tied to Vietnam by language and find adjustment to America quite difficult. Sensitive to Amerasians' need for active support, social services, and the psychological assistance of other refugees, the Mutual Assistance Associations have begun to discuss the problem and some are marginally assisting in the relocation process. It will be the increased activity of these Vietnamese-led and -controlled agencies which will ultimately turn the corner for Amerasians—a corner which needs to be turned quickly, or it will be too late. "We are too slow in helping these [Amerasians]," says an MAA official. "We have to help our people know that they are Vietnamese, too. Really, we are all refugees together. It doesn't matter what else you are."

The Celebration of Têt

Vietnamese refugees in America have continued the observance of ancient holidays from Vietnam. In addition to maintaining celebrations regarding birth, marriage, and ancestors, Vietnamese refugees continue to celebrate Têt. Têt, the Vietnamese New Year, is celebrated on the first day of the first month of the lunar calendar, usually between January 19 and February 20,[24] serving both as a reminder of Vietnamese heritage and as a cohesive factor of identity for the refugee population in a given locality as well as for the whole of communities throughout America.

Têt has historically been the most important holiday in Vietnam. It is the beginning of a new year, and a celebration of the return of spring. Historically, Têt was both a traditional and a religious holiday.[25] For the Vietnamese, it is the equivalent of Thanksgiving Day, Memorial Day, New Year's Day, and birthdays all combined into one massive celebration. As such, it symbolizes new beginnings and the rebirth of the Vietnamese culture. In Vietnam, Têt was a time for paying debts, correcting one's faults, forgiving the errors of others, putting past difficulties beyond you, and making new friends out of old adversaries.

Têt was also a family-centered celebration. In Vietnam, the festivities, which lasted for three days, began in the home. The first day was reserved for family and for paying respects to one's ancestors. The second day was in honor of teachers. Individuals expressed their appreciation for teachers who imparted knowledge and intelligence to them as students. The third day was reserved for visiting friends. It was a day of conversation and reminiscing, usually over food and traditional beverages, and was a day of great merriment. So important was Têt to the Vietnamese people that most families saved throughout the year for the holiday celebration. Houses were repainted and thoroughly cleaned. Flowers and plum branches were used to decorate the homes and large expenses were incurred in the process to insure that the new beginnings were indeed positive ones. Banners inscribed with wishes for happiness, prosperity, and long life was hung in prominent locations both in private residences and in public establishments. In Vietnamese rural areas, Buddhists erected bamboo poles in front of their houses and draped amulets around the poles to repel evil spirits. Flags were flown to attract the spirits of the ancestors, and the traditional Buddhist flag was flown to mark the occasion.

In the United States, Têt has proven to be a major celebration which draws together the old and the new worlds of the refugees. As a time of new beginning, the Vietnamese use the festivities to celebrate their new life in America and point to the future. At the same time that they remember the past, they are keenly aware of the opportunties ahead of them and Têt intangibly has marked the transition from Vietnam to America: it is the community of Vietnamese-Americans remembering the successes of the past as a bridge to the future.

> During Têt, all Vietnamese people bathe the night before. We are showing that we have clean spirits to begin the new cycle and that we rid ourselves of all negative thoughts and all negative forces. It reminds us that we have a clean beginning in America, and that we are together [the Vietnamese community] in our new country. [Lee Tran, Oklahoma City]

For many younger Vietnamese, or for Vietnamese-Americans born in the United States, the celebration is an extrapolation from their parents' background. Many adolescent Vietnamese, who speak English better than Vietnamese, and who are more familiar with American colonial history than with the dynastic histories of Vietnam, think of the celebration as a time for friends, food, and parties.

> I like the Têt celebration. It is a time when we can party and have a good time together. I don't like some of the things with candles, incense, and all that, but I know it is important to my

parents. I don't understand what it all means, but Têt is a way of just being Vietnamese. For my folks it is a way of remembering. For me it is a way of saying that that's kind of a part of me, but so is America. I mean, I am really an American Vietnamese, not an old Vietnamese. [Tran Vo, Midwest city]

Têt is a time of patriotic expression and community. At the beginning of the celebration in the Great Hall at the Myriad in Oklahoma City, the South Vietnamese flag and the American flag are carried forward together prior to the beginning of the speeches, songs, and other performances. A moment of silence is held in memory of both South Vietnamese and American soldiers who died protecting the democratic rights of the people of Vietnam. Prayers for the nation of Vietnam and the United States are offered and the national anthems of both countries are sung. Remembrances such as this commemorating the relationship of Vietnam and America take place not only in the Great Hall, but also in ceremonies at the Cathedral of Our Lady of Perpetual Help, a Roman Catholic Church, and at Giac Quang Temple, a Buddhist temple. The cultural aspects of Têt effectively help the people to bridge their past and their present and establish a clear vision for the future.

Têt, as important as it is, is not the only celebration brought from Vietnam and adapted to a new society. In Carthage, Missouri, the Fathers of the Congregation of the Mother Co-Redemptrix, a Vietnamese religious order, host the celebration of Marian Days. Marian Days is a time of thanksgiving for the deliverance of the Vietnamese; a time which now includes thanksgiving for the safe travel and arrival of Vietnamese refugees to America.[26] Marian Days, like Têt, transcends refugee generations, and older persons, often dressed traditionally, walk side by side with younger Vietnamese in bluejeans and Nikes. This festival with food, large numbers of old friends, and a religious foundation serves for many Vietnamese as a means of continuity from ancient customs to newly adopted and adapted patterns. It combines the old and the new, and reflects the changes within the refugee community; changes which are forming the foundation for contemporary Vietnamese-American society.

VII

CONTEMPORARY VIETNAMESE-AMERICAN SOCIETY

The evolving and developing Vietnamese refugee communities within the United States have not taken final shape, and will undoubtedly undergo continuing change for the foreseeable future. Nevertheless, following the first fifteen years of resettlement in America, patterns have emerged which give insight into the diachronically emerging characteristics of Vietnamese-American populations, and which underscore the formulation of contemporary refugee society.

Stability and Fluidity

The stability of Vietnamese refugee communities remains rooted in the family. In Southeast Asia, family, including extended kinship, is not simply one social principle of society, it is perhaps *the* foundation of social structure. When one needs assistance, he or she may always go to the family, and the family will unilaterally give support. Aid from blood relatives is mandatory, and reciprocity within the family is standard. This support system, which was fragmented by the U.S. government's policy of diffusing refugees throughout the various states for resettlement, is the primary reason for secondary migration within the United States. Individuals and nuclear families are moving from places of initial settlement to urban centers in order to join their relatives. Should a refugee not be able to locate blood relatives, secondary migration remains the pattern as refugees search for areas where other Vietnamese-Americans are settling. Refugees relocating to regional ethnic centers are sometimes identified within the Vietnamese community as fictive kin (adopted kin), and Vietnamese are assuming kin relations based on the commonality of experience and ethnicity.

To further insure the stability of family, Vietnamese-American communities are pooling their resources to help family members in holding camps overseas make their way to America. Money is collected at celebrations, selected worship services, and special fund drives. MAAs coordinate the effort to locate relatives, and administer the money through appropriate agencies and volunteer assistance groups. As new persons arrive, the community takes shape in accordance with their family status, economic ability, and political influence. The family, then, is both a stabilizing influence on refugees and simultaneously a fluid institution allowing for change without losing societal equilibrium.

Stabilization is also found in the growing expression of religion in America. Vietnamese Catholic congregations made the transition with relative ease since Roman Catholicism is prominent in America and ethnic priests were welcomed into local parishes by the resident priests. Even to Americans who viewed the refugees suspiciously and ethnocentrically, Catholicism was acceptable as a "Western" and Christian religion. Buddhists were not as readily accepted, but in the intervening fifteen years, the various successes of Vietnamese-Americans and the increasing cultural contact between the refugees and other Americans have resulted in renewed tolerance. In addition, some localities such as Hacienda Heights, a suburb of Los Angeles, had already zoned property for churches and included in the definition of church Buddhist temples. As a result, a $14 million Chinese Buddhist temple, the largest temple in the United States, built on fifteen acres, was completed in 1989. This Buddhist presence, which predated the arrival of refugees in 1975, had already laid the groundwork for Vietnamese-Buddhist expressions and provided freedom in California which was much more difficult to achieve in other states. To assist with societal acceptance and understanding of Buddhism, the Vietnamese Buddhist Temple in Los Angeles[1] published a book entitled *The Presence of Vietnamese Buddhists in America* on the occasion of the Buddha's 2,525th birthday in May 1981. Copies of the book were given to Vietnamese temples across America and to any interested parties. The goal as stated in the book was to achieve a "greater culture-religious interchange between Vietnamese and Americans."[2] This has provided for Vietnamese refugees a form of stability which could not be achieved in any other manner. There is simply no substitute for the family or for religious expression in establishing community and stability for Vietnamese people.

The transition period since 1975 has shown the ingenuity of refugee peoples. In adjusting to American society, there has been a conscious effort to inform and educate Americans about Vietnamese society at the same time that refugees were learning and adjusting to the United States. During Tết celebrations, Americans are invited to participate and ushers insure that someone hosts the guests and explains the ceremonies. Buddhist temples are conducting not only worship services but services of meditation that appeal to many Americans and drawing Americanized Vietnamese children who find this more acceptable than the traditional religion. In Houston, the Hidden Valley Vietnamese Church has begun a thirty-minute television program, and became the first Protestant congregation to make use of American media for evangelism with the consent and help of local pastors. Conversations leading up to the television agreement necessitated an exchange of both culture and religion among the interested parties.

Stability has also meant a greater participation in Vietnamese-American activities by longer-term Americans and a reciprocal participation by Vietnamese in more mainstream American activities. For instance, when the Buddhist temple opened in Beaumont, Texas, the mayor and city dignitaries were prominent in the ceremonies along with the Buddhist monks. Local ads were placed in the newspaper, and television reporters were on the scene to interview and record the event. In Oklahoma City, the Vietnamese community raised $4,378 for the families of three firefighters, two of whom were killed and one of whom was injured, while fighting a fire on March 8, 1989.[3] The fund was promoted by *Viet Bao*, an Oklahoma City Vietnamese newspaper, and the fund raising effort drew praise from many parts of the city. In Southern California, the opening of a Vietnamese restaurant or grocery store is a cause for celebration for the local Chamber of Commerce, and in St. Louis, stories designed to inform residents about Vietnamese refugees are appearing in the local press, written from a highly favorable point of view.[4]

The associations between refugee and more settled communities are not limited to education, protocol, and public relations. The Vietnamese refugees have established relationships with, and sought the assistance of, a number of professional organizations who are fully engaged with the refugee communities. In New York, the Lawyers Committee for Human Rights has become involved in the forced repatriation of Vietnamese refugees from Hong Kong to Vietnam. A court challenge to the refugee screening process of Hong Kong's camp officials which was brought in April 1990 has been supported by the LCHR, as well as by the UNHCR. Local builders and realtors in Houston have worked alongside refugees in starting business enterprises such as shopping centers, video stores, and the merchandising of Asian products. In Seattle, the proliferation of entrepreneurial ventures by Vietnamese has made them more than compatible with local consumers, and in Dallas, a Vietnamese cultural center is on the drawing board which will represent Vietnamese culture to Americans and provide employment and economic expansion within the region.

Economically and culturally the Vietnamese communities have constructed a solid path for other refugees to follow, and are envisioning the direction further paths will take in the future. The one destabilizing influence that remains is politics: politics relating primarily to Vietnam and to the process of establishing relations with the Socialist Republic of Vietnam. The deep division among refugees on this issue may be seen in the violence which has sporadically erupted as a result of opposing views. In Fresno, California, in August 1989, Doan Van Toai, a writer and advocate of improving relations with the Vietnamese Communist government, was shot and critically wounded. The assailants could have been idealogues from the right or the left, or simply opponents of normalizing relations for whatever reason.[5] Staunchly anti-communist in composition, many Vietnamese communities have contributed to a fund which is directed at supporting insurgents in Vietnam. Realistically not expecting to overthrow the Hanoi government, they are nevertheless determined to destabilize, if possible, and certainly to harass the government that drove them from their country. Anyone who gives the appearance of sympathizing with normalization could be subject to assassination, arson, and threats directed at their family.

As inflexible as this position remains for many refugees, fluidity among the communities is visible everywhere. Families from Honolulu are now allowed and even encouraged to return to Vietnam for brief visits with in-country relatives. Language which has been and remains very difficult for later arrivals is now being taught by native Vietnamese-language instructors who better understand the difficulties in the linguistic transition. Mobility among families is increasing as affluence develops for a few, and the sense of responsibility among Vietnamese for other refugees is accelerating the adjustment process. Religion, used as a cultural bridge and as a form of self-identity, is increasingly adapting its structures to fit American forms, and educational opportunities, especially among the young, are opening up American enterprise. Resilient in their ability to survive, Vietnamese-Americans are stabilizing within their communities while avoiding rigidity. The fluidity of the process of adaptation has kept the community in a cycle of growth culturally, spiritually, and economically.

An Emerging Model of Adaptation

Extensive studies of Japanese-American and Chinese-American communities have been conducted by social scientists, but to date few models of acculturation, assimilation, or adaptation have been constructed regarding the Vietnamese. Since large numbers of Vietnamese entered the United States only fifteen years ago, and the initial emphasis was on assisting refugees in securing shelter, food, and employment, social scientists are only now assessing the Vietnamese-American populations to investigate patterns of resettlement.

Historically, the Vietnamese have had to adjust to invaders within their country and to forced migrations as a result of outside domination. Documentation shows that the Vietnamese have resisted outside influences and sought to maintain their own identity in spite of overwhelming odds. From 111 B.C. to 939 A.D., the Chinese dominated Vietnam and forged aspects of Sinification into the Vietnamese societal framework. The Vietnamese, however, even over this extensive period, remained recalcitrant, as is evidenced by the Vietnamese language. During this thousand-year period, the Chinese introduced their writing system and sought to substitute it for Vietnamese, but the Vietnamese people retained the non-Sinitic foundation of spoken Vietnamese in spite of the addition of Chinese loan words. Shortly after the Chinese withdrew in 939 A.D., the language was romanized as a sign of the continuing and unique natural character of Vietnam.

The adjustment of the Vietnamese into the United States has taken on characteristics similar to those of their ancestors who resisted Chinese acculturation. Involving social and psychological adjustments, contact with new moral and spiritual standards that conflict with traditional belief systems can be quite unstabilizing. The foundational principles of one's societal structure and the philosophy upon which it is based are forced to undergo radical scrutiny within a prevailing culture that generally neither recognizes nor understands the "opposing" philosophy. The abrupt nature of this submergence has created mental health problems, confusion as to cultural identity, and serious conflicts in resettlement for immigrant groups not only in America but in other countries as well.

The Vietnamese, however, with a historical precedence for resiliency, have managed to overcome much of the difficulty involved in culture shock, and problems related to refugee communities are often a result of forced withdrawal from their native culture in addition to coping with a new society. It is difficult to isolate any single group of Asian-Americans and from that group's settlement experience superimpose upon Vietnamese refugees a similar model. Rather than identify with Japanese-American, Chinese-American, Filipino-American, or Korean-American processes, the Vietnamese have carved out a model of their own. The model involves adaptation, resistance, and retention.

The Vietnamese model does not preclude American influence; in fact, quite the contrary. Vietnamese-Americans are experiencing influences in the area of family, gender roles, economics, and individual freedoms. As these influences begin to penetrate more traditional Vietnamese cultural patterns, Vietnamese-Americans do not tend to discard former customs, nor do they ignore or refuse to engage the new cultural standards. On the contrary, the refugees have learned to succeed through the use of cultural elements as a catalyst to that success. Bridging the Chinese and Japanese models, the Vietnamese have effectively maintained the viability of both indigenous and host cultural units, viewing them neither as constituents nor opponents, but rather as necessary co-ingredients for survival. This syncretistic position is easily identifiable in Vietnamese religious history, as are the processes of adaptability through the traditional systems of Confucianism, Taoism, and Buddhism.

There are forms of the host society which the refugees have rejected. Particular customs and behaviors viewed as threats to their self-identity, self-esteem, or societal cohesiveness are rejected outright. The Vietnamese have historically been a fiercely independent people with an intense degree of ethnic identity. As viewed in the Chinese occupation, the Vietnamese were never reticent about resisting cultural capitulation, and primary social institutions such as family, and religion were protected from foundational change.[6] In the United States, the tendency toward secondary migration to ethnic enclaves and the formation of community organizations as bulwarks of security provides the refugees with psychological fortresses necessary to resist negatively construed cultural components. With tools for achieving the maintenance of traditional social patterns, the Vietnamese have, in a premeditated strategy, elected not to become isolationists. Although they may choose to reject certain prevailing standards of the host culture, they do not withdraw but continue strong interaction with, and within, American society.

The third aspect of the emergent Vietnamese model of resettlement is the retention of old-world values.[7] To be sure, the degree of retention corresponds on a diminishing ratio to increasingly younger age groups, but it exists across the board. As a facilitator and depository of culture and heritage, language is viewed as primary in adaptation. In Vietnamese-American homes, the Vietnamese language is spoken and is not replaced by English. Traditional ceremonies, religious festivals, and community celebrations are supported with the same fervor as they may have been in Southeast Asia. The retention of traditional customs is viewed by Vietnamese refugees as an act of self-identity and reverence for the past, not as a pattern of mandated nonconformity to American society. It retains the basic elements of the "self" without discrediting the definitions of "self" woven throughout the American mosaic. In an article entitled "Vietnamese Immigrants and Their Adjustment to American Society" in *Dat Moi* magazine [New Land], Le Xuan Khoa wrote, "We can demand to be equal, but we cannot and should not want to be alike."

Vietnamese-Americans have chosen a course which cannot be definitively described as either acculturation or assimilation. Denotative concepts of these patterns simply do not fit the Vietnamese experience in America. Instead, the Vietnamese have orchestrated a Vietnamese image of Vietnamese-Americans which they hold out to American society. To that extent, they retain aspects of their heritage and invite Americans to appreciate their background and history. Simultaneously, Vietnamese refugees have adapted to a new environment and to newly introduced cultural aspects of their host society, while maintaining a strong sense of self-identity and self-esteem. This model of "cultural integrity and adaptation" weaves together selected elements of the American culture necessary for survival, achievement, and future success, while preserving traditional values and belief systems underscoring an intense and proud ethnic heritage.

Achievement in America

The trip to the United States involved numerous hardships, and the adjustments to a new society have not been without difficulties. With these aspects of the Vietnamese experience well documented, and with studies concerning the number of years spent on welfare rolls and in the public assistance corridor, the achievements of refugees in America have often gone unnoticed. Quietly and methodically, Vietnamese-Americans are beginning to make a mark on American society as a whole, well beyond the boundaries of their localized communities.

In the national arena, the Bush administration in 1988 appointed a Vietnamese woman, Mary Chi Ray, as Deputy Director of the Office of Refugee Resettlement. She had formerly chaired Asian-American Nationals for Bush 88, a Republican group supporting the Bush nomination. In Illinois, Governor Jim Thompson has appointed Ngoan Le as Special Assistant on Asian American Affairs, where she will work as a special liaison between the state government and Asian-Americans.[8]

Entrepreneurs within the refugee community are also impacting larger communities with publications, the prospect for jobs, and the influence of their ideas. A monthly newsletter, *Asian Business and Community News*, is published by Nghi Huynh in Minnesota, a state with a sizable refugee population.[9] Dr. David Vu in Oklahoma City publishes *Viet Bao*, a newspaper initially designed for Vietnamese language readers but which now is expanding to include English language users as well. In Dallas, Hiep Thai Dang publishes *Ban Nguyet San Thoi Dam* (New Forum), a bimonthly magazine with roughly twice the number of pages as *Newsweek*.[10] Beginning with a small circulation, the magazine has grown to have a subscription of approximately 4,000 and is currently soliciting and drawing advertisements from long-term local businesses in Dallas, Arlington, and Fort Worth.

Educationally, Vietnamese refugees are succeeding at an exponential rate. In 1985, Jean Nguyen and Hung Vu became the first Vietnamese to graduate from the U.S. Military Academy at West Point,[11] and Tue Nguyen, only nine years after arriving in America, earned his seventh degree in 1988, a Ph.D. in nuclear engineering from the Massachusetts Institute of Technology.[12] Tu Anh Ngoc Tran, who arrived in the United States at the age of fourteen with no knowledge of English, graduated at the age of sixteen as valedictorian of her class of 350 students at Lanier High School in Austin, Texas.[13] The success of Vietnamese-Americans in high schools and universities across America forecasts the benefits gained from the resettlement of refugee peoples. Within a short period of time, the costs necessitated in the resettlement process will be overshadowed by the financial benefits, both direct and indirect, derived from the contributions made to the economic development of America by refugee-Americans.

Vietnamese-Americans are also achieving success in society. Measured not only in economic terms, but in the reality that refugees are surviving the resettlement process and growing stronger daily, the refugees bring value intangibles which benefit the whole of American society. Family-oriented, self-sufficient, and resilient by nature, Vietnamese-Americans possess a determination to succeed and the disciplined will to achieve that success. Spiritual leaders encourage their people to continue the fight to succeed and to live independently. Father Anthony Bao of Our Lady's Cathedral Parish in Oklahoma City, Reverend Ha Nguyen of the Faith Baptist Church in Dallas, and the High Honorable One of the Vietnamese Buddhist Temple in Oklahoma have all served as inspirational leaders for the followers of their faiths. When the battle seems overwhelming the spirit of these leaders, along with the spirit of their communities, proves to be more than adequate in helping refugees keep going.

> I know that for my children to do well in America, I must do
> well, also. And when I am, as you say in America, feeling
> down, it is my church which keeps me going. It is the place of
> my faith, and my heritage. It is my place of comfort. [Viet-
> namese father, Oklahoma City]

The achievements of Vietnamese-Americans are not relegated to one particular area or one particular sector of American life. A growing diversity within the community and the
prospect for increasing contributions to the American future
are evident in the success of refugees in a variety of fields.
Xuong Nguyen-huu is a Professor of Physics, Chemistry and
Biology at the University of California at San Diego, Hung
Nguyen and Hoc Lam are proprietors of a Vietnamese restaurant in Minneapolis–St. Paul,[14] and Nguyen Anh Nga is a
psychiatrist with the University of Oklahoma Medical
School. Entrepreneurs have begun their own businesses, from
grocery stores to insurance companies, and have clienteles
which represent the major ethnic groups of the cities in which
they are prospering. For a population which only began
entering the United States fifteen years ago, the Vietnamese
are achieving economic stability (as evidenced and discussed
earlier in chapter 5), cultural continuity and adjustment (as
viewed in chapter 6), and growing success in the American
mosaic. Their presence will be a strengthening factor in the
fabric of the American future.

The Outlook for the Future

The entrance of Vietnamese refugees into the United States
remains a relatively recent event, and the establishment of a
Vietnamese-American identity is continuing. Unfortunately,
as one looks to the future and sees inevitable and positive
change, one also sees a disturbing continuation of persistent
problems. The future will be mixed: bright for many established refugee peoples, continuously traumatic for others,
and in a state of flux and change for all.

After years of tragedy and difficulty, the prospect for boat
people leaving Vietnam is not encouraging. The most op-

timistic projections forecast a continuing exodus from mainland Southeast Asia, a diminishing welcome for refugees in countries of first asylum, increased attacks by pirates in the South China Sea and the Gulf of Thailand, and evaporating aid from westernized countries who have entered a state of assistance fatigue. The United Nations High Commission for Refugees perseveres in their attempt to aid refugees, but their budgets and manpower, in relation to the demand all over the world, are near exhaustion. Simplistic answers abound, but the problem of the refugees is not so easily solved. Programs such as the Orderly Departure Program will spearhead efforts at solutions, and the complexity of this and other humanitarian needs is now being addressed by national governments. Whether or not the intellectual solutions can match the pragmatic needs of budgets, human resources, and political will to meet the needs, remains to be seen.

Within the Vietnamese-American communities in the United States, gradual change will persevere through the next several generations. As Jesse Nash points out in his paper "Current Research on Asian-Americans on the Gulf Coast,"

> the Vietnamese community is a place of often intense conflict. The conflicts are those between generations, the sexes, class sections, and linguistic interests, that is, those who want Vietnamese alone spoken in the community and those who want more English spoken. The community though, because of its strong bonding in communal structures, is not torn apart by these conflicts. The conflicts actually provide a forum whereby the community can make decisions as to its future. In a very real sense, everything in the Vietnamese community is up for grabs and is open to discussion.[15]

Vietnamese elders have carefully crafted the establishment of a Vietnamese image in the United States, and are careful that their resettlement takes a positive course not only for the refugees, but for all Americans as well. Both within the community and without, the Vietnamese-American leadership always seeks a harmonious consensus before proceeding. The strength of the community is revitalized and never undercut when deliberations concerning the future are discussed. As Nash observes, "Where the Vietnamese differ from some other groups I have worked with is that the discussions are almost always civil. To belong to the community itself is valued and this provides a buffer against extremism."[16]

As the Vietnamese-American population grows numerically and economically, it will increasingly play a role in the shaping of the American future. Refugees who have elected to live in close proximity to persons of similar ethnicity are also slowly beginning to increase their participation in mainstream society. Vietnamese are purchasing homes in traditional neighborhoods, serving on the volunteer agendas of local communities, and simultaneously assisting new refugees through the MAAs. They are bridging both societies and helping to create a new one in the process.

Perhaps a recent event at the Buddhist Temple in Oklahoma City best illustrates the future for refugees who are both Vietnamese and American. Following the Buddhist service, dinner was held on the grounds, and I noticed that a young friend of mine, an 11-year-old girl, was sitting on the grass outside the Temple eating with several friends. As I approached, they invited me to join them, and I did so. She and I were both eating egg rolls, but whereas I was using chopsticks, I noticed that she was using a fork. On my plate was soy sauce, on hers, ketchup. When I asked her why she had literally covered her egg roll in ketchup, which is not traditionally Vietnamese, she answered proudly, "I do it like this because I am an American!"

APPENDIX

Basic Vietnamese Customs

1. The family is the basis of society, not the individual.
2. Three to four generations may reside together in one home.
3. Within the family, the wife deals with all household matters. The husband deals with the outside world (the family is patriarchal).
4. The elderly (parents) are supported by married or unmarried children until they die.
5. Names are written as follows: Family name, Middle name, Given name, e.g., Nguyen Van Hai. The family name is placed first as an emphasis on the person's heritage.
6. Family members use different given names.
7. A large family is traditional.
8. Children reside with their parents until marriage. The males marry between the ages of 20 and 30, while the females marry between the ages of 18 and 25.
9. The marriages must be approved by the parents of both the male and female. This is true regardless of ages. (Not a legal requirement, but a traditional one.)
10. First cousins and their children cannot marry each other up to three generations.
11. The celebration of marriage is preferred in the home of one of the marriage participants, not in a church or temple.
12. Legally, women keep their own names after marriage. Formally, married women use their husband's name.
    Example

Husband's name	Nguyen Van Hai
Wife's maiden name	Le Thi Ba
Wife's married name	Le Thi Ba
Wife's formal name	Mrs. Nguyen Van Hai

13. After marriage, the wife lives with her husband's family. She is considered to "belong" to her husband's family.
14. Before 1959, Vietnamese men could have multiple wives (polygyny). Ranking developed according to responsibility among the wives. Following entrance into the U.S., only one spouse remains married to the husband and second or subsequent marriages may be dissolved. Wives are still informally accepted as family in U.S.
15. When a child is born, it is considered one year old.

153

16. Sons are more highly valued than daughters.
17. The eldest son has a duty to perform the ancestor worship at home.
18. Brothers and sisters do not touch or kiss one another.
19. If a parent dies, the children customarily wait three years before marrying.
20. If a wife dies, the husband must wait one year before remarrying.
21. If a sibling dies, the others must wait one year to marry.
22. To show respect, Vietnamese will bow their heads in front of a superior or aged person.
23. While conversing, one should not look steadily at a respected person's eyes.
24. Women do not shake hands with each other or with men.
25. Women do not smoke in public.
26. Vietnamese never touch another's head. Only the elderly can touch the head of a young child.
27. Summoning a person with a hand or finger in an up position is reserved only for animals or inferior persons. Between two equal people, it is a provocation. To summon an individual, the entire hand with fingers facing downward is the only appropriate hand signal.
28. Persons of the same sex may hold hands in public and/or sleep in the same bed without public derision.
29. Incest is punished by law and strongly resented by society.
30. The concept of equality between the sexes is the same as in Western countries, but socially man is still considered slightly superior to woman.
31. The symbol of nationhood (Vietnamese) is the yellow dragon. Yellow is the color of royalty. The dragon symbolizes descent of the Vietnamese from the mythical dragon.

Source: Compiled from interviews with various Vietnamese persons residing in Oklahoma City and from Vuong G. Thuy, *Getting to Know the Vietnamese and Their Culture.*

AMERICAN AND VIETNAMESE PHILOSOPHY COMPARED

Item	Americans	Vietnamese
Human nature orientation	Human nature is basically evil but perfectible	Human nature is basically good but corruptible
Man-nature orientation	Mastery over nature	Harmony between man and nature
Time orientation	Living with future time	Living with the past
Space orientation	Living with movement, migration, and mobility	Attached to nature or ancestor's land—immobile
Activity orientation	Doing, getting things done	Being-in-becoming
Relation orientation	Individual autonomy, self-reliance	Lineality, mutual dependence

Adapted from Nguyen Quoc Tri, "Culture and Technical Assistance in Public Administration: A Study of What Can Be Transferred from the United States to Vietnam." Ph.D. dissertation, University of Southern California, 1970.

NOTES

1. The Vietnamese Entrance into America

1. Paul Rutledge, *A Bridge to Freedom* (Shawnee, Oklahoma: Ethnographic Research Lab Monograph No. 1, 1986). Other sources include Bernard Fall, *The Two Vietnams* (London: Pall Mall Press, 1963); Joseph Buttinger, *The Smaller Dragon* (New York: Praeger, 1958); Frances FitzGerald, *Fire in the Lake: The Vietnamese and the Americans in Vietnam* (Boston: Little, Brown, 1971); and Edgar O'Ballance, *The Wars in Vietnam, 1954–1980* (New York: Hippocrene Books, 1981).

2. Interviews conducted with military personnel while living in Hawaii who participated in the evacuation of Saigon. Additional interviews with refugees indicated a similar perspective.

3. Conversation with military personnel, U.S. Marine Corps. Also, a good historical discussion is found in Keith St. Cartmail's *Exodus Indochina* (New Zealand: Heinemann Publishers, 1983).

4. U.S. Department of State records document thoroughly the communications which occurred during the last days of Saigon.

5. Darrel Montero, *Vietnamese-Americans: Patterns of Resettlement and Socioeconomic Adaptation in the United States* (Boulder, Colorado: Westview Press, 1979).

6. Paul Rutledge, *The Role of Religion in Ethnic Self-Identity: A Vietnamese Community* (Lanham, Maryland: University Press of America, 1985).

7. Interviews with Vietnamese-Americans and with community leaders in Houston.

8. Rutledge, *The Role of Religion in Ethnic Self-Identity.*

9. Diana Miserez, *Refugees: The Trauma of Exile* (Dordrecht, Netherlands: Martinus Nijhoff, 1988).

10. Phillip Bennaum, Robert Bennaum, and Paula Kelly, *The Peoples from Indo-China* (Victoria, Australia: Hodja Educational Resources Cooperative, 1984).

11. Ibid.

12. *Refugee and Immigrant Resource Directory* is an excellent source of continuing data on newly arrived peoples in America. The 1990–91 edition was published by the Denali Press, Juneau, Alaska.

13. Deborah Anker, *The Law of Asylum in the United States: A Manual for Practitioners and Adjudicators* (Washington, D.C.: American Immigration Lawyers Association, 1989).

14. Rutledge, *The Role of Religion in Ethnic Self-Identity*.

15. Ibid.

16. Ibid.

17. Netnapis Nakavachara and John Rogge, "Thailand's Refugee Experience," in John Rogge, ed., *Refugees: A Third World Dilemma* (Totowa, New Jersey: Rowman and Littlefield, 1987); *Refugee Reports*, January 1988; "Getting Tough with Boat People," *Asiaweek*, February 26, 1988, p. 21; *Indochina Journal*, Spring 1988; *The New Straits Times*, November 29, 1978; St. Cartmail, *Exodus Indochina*, p. 223; Report to the Congress of the United States by the Comptroller General, April 24, 1979. The report was entitled *The Indochinese Exodus: A Humanitarian Dilemma*.

18. St. Cartmail, *Exodus Indochina*, pp. 223, 246–248; *Merdeka Newspaper*, July 31, 1979.

19. *Asiaweek*, August 23, 1987.

20. *Singapore Government Population Bulletin*, 1988.

21. Paul Rutledge and Richard Ady, *Dong Duong Di Tan* (Indochina Exodus) (Los Alamitas, California: Ban Xuan Thu Publishers, 1992).

22. "Indochinese Refugee Activity," *Refugee Reports*, December 16, 1988; St. Cartmail, *Exodus Indochina*. Leonard Davis, "Hong Kong and the Indochinese Refugees," in Supang Chantavanich and E. Bruce Reynolds, eds., *Indochinese Refugees: Asylum and Resettlement* (Bangkok: Institute of Asian Studies, Chulalongkorn University, 1988). Information was also obtained from interviews with assistance officials.

23. "Vietnamese Refugees in China," *Refugees*, United Nations High Commission for Refugees, January 1985; Zhu Rong, "China and the Indochinese Refugees," in Chantavanich and Reynolds, *Indochinese Refugees*.

24. Supang Chantavanich, "Japan and the Indochinese Refugees," in Chantavanich and Reynolds, *Indochinese Refugees*. See also chart, "Southeast Asian Refugee Arrivals in the United States and Other Countries," U.S. Department of State, 1988.

2. Emigration to the United States

1. Since 1975, when I first began to work with refugee people while living in Hawaii, I have been gathering their stories and insights. As of 1990, many remain reticent about having their names attached to their experiences due to family members remaining in Vietnam, the fear of public embarrassment in this country should their point of view not be well received, and the general reluctance to be "seen" while continuing to settle in the United States. Many are moving out of the shadows, but others remain reluctant. As a compromise, a number of my informants have allowed me to use one of their names, but not their full names.

3. Initial Resettlement

1. Deborah Anker, *The Law of Asylum in the United States: A Manual for Practitioners and Adjudicators* (Washington, D.C.: American Immigration Lawyers Association, 1983).

2. Source: United States Refugee Act of 1980, published by the U.S. Congress.

3. Interview with Mr. Thu, President of the Vietnamese-American Association, Oklahoma City, 1983.

4. Paul Rutledge, "The Vietnamese Tradition through Kailua, Hawaii: A Personal and Historical Perspective," *East Asia Journal of Theology*, Hong Kong, Vol. 1, No. 2, October 1983.

5. *Refugees*, United Nations High Commission for Refugees, December 1985, p. 13.

6. *Daily Oklahoman*, Friday, April 17, 1981.

7. *National Geographic*, "Troubled Odyssey of Vietnamese Fishermen," September 1981, p. 387.

8. "Fish or Foul? Refugee Fishermen in California," *Refugees*, December 1984, p. 33.

9. Paul Starr, "Troubled Waters: Vietnamese Fisherfolk on America's Gulf Coast," *International Migration Review*, Vol. 15, No. 1, Spring-Summer, 1981.

10. *The Daily Oklahoman*, Monday, May 14, 1990, p. 5, Associated Press Informational Release.

11. The source for the flier reproduced and the other particulars is the Southeast Asian Community Development Foundation, 875 O'Farrell Street, San Francisco, California, 94109.

12. Paul Rutledge, "Traditional Patterns and Belief Organizations: The Prognosis for Vietnamese Acculturation and Assimilation in the United States," *Asian Journal of Theology*, Singapore, Spring 1988.

13. An excellent book to pursue the Indianization of Southeast Asia is G. Coedes, *The Indianized States of Southeast Asia* (Honolulu: University Press of Hawaii, 1971).

14. Paul Rutledge, *The Role of Religion in Ethnic Self-Identity: A Vietnamese Community* (Lanham, Md.:, University Press of America, 1985), pp. 32–34.

15. Ibid., pp. 26–28.

16. Ibid., p. 27.

17. Donald N. Brown, *The Vietnamese-American Experience in Oklahoma* (Stillwater: College of Arts and Sciences, Oklahoma State University, 1981).

18. Interview with Father Anthony Bao, Oklahoma City, 1986.

19. Ibid., p. 39.

20. Ibid., p. 39.

21. *Dallas Morning News*, January 31, 1988, announcement of the Temple Dedication.

22. Personal experience at the Buddhist Temple, Oklahoma City.

23. Conversation with the High Venerable One, Oklahoma, 1982.

24. Phone conversation with Sister Marlosh, 1982.

25. Notes from the conference on "Indochinese Refugees Resettlement and Adjustment," 1981. Lecture by Dr. Vuong Gia Thuy of Temple University, Philadelphia, Pennsylvania.

26. This practice of singing the National Anthem has diminished in regularity as the resettlement of refugees continues over a long period of time.

27. Personal conversation and interview with Multicultural Community Center Director, counselors and volunteers, May 1990.

28. Conversation with Mr. Thu Suong Tran, Dallas, May, 1990.

29. Conversation with Mr. Nguyen Ro, Coordinator of the Vietnamese Elderly Association of Dallas, May, 1990.

30. Problem discussed with elders of various Vietnamese communities. Anyone may visit an MAA and get information on its programs and services. In most instances, the executives on staff are more than eager to explain their problems to you and talk with you concerning what their agency provides for the community.

4. The Vietnamese-American Community

1. *Oklahoma Today*, a monthly magazine, has on occasion published some material on the Oklahoma City Vietnamese. Generally the articles are on customs and values and serve to further introduce the residents of Oklahoma to Vietnamese-Americans.

2. Paul Rutledge, experience in Oklahoma, 1980.

3. *Sociology and Social Research*, XVIII: 340–350, published in 1934.

4. Paul Rutledge, "Traditional Patterns and Belief Organizations: The Prognosis for Vietnamese Acculturation and Assimilation in the United States," *Asian Journal of Theology*, Singapore, Spring 1988.

5. Le Xuan Khoa, "Vietnamese Immigrants and Their Adjustment to American Society," paper presented at the Conference for IRAP grantees and contractors, D.H.E.W. Region II, New Jersey, April 1979.

6. During the past fifteen years, I have been privileged to visit in several hundred Vietnamese-American homes and observe the developing patterns.

7. The United Nations High Commission for Refugees has consistently led the relief efforts for all Vietnamese refugees, including boat people.

8. Information obtained from the U.S. State Department and obtained in correspondence with Senator Don Nickles, Oklahoma, April, 1987.

9. Judith Strauch, *The Chinese Exodus from Vietnam: Im-*

plications for the Southeast Asian Chinese, Occasional Paper No. 1, Cultural Survival, Cambridge, Massachusetts, December 1980.

10. B. Martin Tsamenyi, "The 'Boat People': Are They Refugees?" *Human Rights Quarterly* (Baltimore: Johns Hopkins University Press), Vol. 5, No. 3, August 1983.

11. Information release, United Nations High Commission for Refugees, 1979.

12. Letter from Senator David Boren, Oklahoma, March 28, 1986.

13. Ibid.

14. Ibid.

15. Information obtained from letter written by James W. Dyer, Acting Assistant Secretary, Legislative and Intergovernmental Affairs, to Senator David Boren of Oklahoma, regarding materials and information requested by Paul Rutledge. March 28, 1986.

16. U.S. Department of State Bureau for Refugee Program, *World Refugee Report,* September 1987, p. 11.

17. *The Bridge,* December 1988, p. 15.

5. Societal Integration and Adjustment

1. Fred von der Mehden, *The Ethnic Groups of Houston* (Houston: Rice University Press, 1984, p. 95).

2. Vietnamese-American Association Survey and subsequent interview with Mr. Thu, President, 1982.

3. *The Daily Oklahoman,* Monday, May 2, 1988, p. 4.

4. See the Office of Refugee Resettlement reports for 1986 and 1987. Also, 1982, Spring Survey, Vietnamese-American Survey, Oklahoma City.

5. Personal experience based on interviews at the market. In addition, the *St. Louis Post-Dispatch,* February 19, 1990, Business Plus Section, had some information on the Ethnic grocery stores in St. Louis.

6. *Daily Oklahoman,* May 2, 1988, p. 4, "Friendly Food Convenience Stores."

7. "Refugees: Stung by a Backlash," *U.S. News and World Report,* October 13, 1980, p. 63.

8. Charles H. Mindel, Robert W. Habenstein, and Roosevelt Wright, Jr., *Ethnic Families in America: Patterns and Variations* (New York: Elsevier, 1988), pp. 276–302.

9. Charles Muzny, "The Vietnamese in Oklahoma City: A Study in Ethnic Change" (Ph.D. dissertation, University of Oklahoma, 1985), p. 104.

10. Orange County Government Documents, 1986.

11. *Refugee and Immigrant Resource Directory,* Appendix A, p. 195.

12. Ibid., p. 195.

13. Statistical data provided by U.S. Department of Health and Human Services, Office of Refugee Resettlement, 1984.

14. "Do-It-Yourself Financing," *Time,* July 25, 1988, p. 62.
15. Conversation with Dr. Jesse Nash, Loyola University, at the Southwest Conference for Asian Studies, Southern Methodist University, 1987.
16. Paul Rutledge, *The Role of Religion in Ethnic Self-Identity: A Vietnamese Community* (Lanham, Md.: University Press of America, 1985), pp. 26–29.
17. Phillip Bennoun, Robert Bennoun and Paula Kelly, *The Peoples from Indo-China* (Victoria: Hodja Educational Resources Cooperative, 1984).
18. Conference on Indo-chinese Refugees, Oklahoma City, 1982.
19. Interview of Dr. Thuong Nguyen in the *Sunday Oklahoman,* May 1, 1988.
20. Chris Brawley, "Education Gets Focus of Family," *Sunday Oklahoman,* May 1, 1988, front page, early bird edition.
21. *Time,* "The New Whiz Kids," by David Brand, August 31, 1987, p. 42.
22. Ibid., 42–43.
23. Vietnamese elders have tried to plan strategies whereby they can assist new arrivals with home mortgages. The continued desire to house under one roof the extended family has created some problems, but that is dissipating as families adopt the concept of single family dwellings.
24. Numerous conversations with leaders in Dallas, Oklahoma City, Seattle, and Southern California have all touched on the personal loans made by the community to refugee members. The practice is relatively widespread.
25. Conversation with medical practitioner in Dallas. A number of articles are also available on traditional healing practices of Southeast Asia generally, and on those practices which relate to Vietnam specifically.
26. *Phong* is a concept difficult to fully grasp by non-Vietnamese or Western persons. Several Buddhist-healing practitioners have explained the idea to me, and I continue to read material available in an attempt to more fully understand the philosophical base upon which it rests.
27. Rutledge, discussion of folk concepts of Taoism, *The Role of Religion in Ethnic Self-Identity,* p. 30.
28. Some refugees have not abandoned the idea of supernatural causes, but say that modern medicine addresses those causes indirectly rather than directly. Many, however, continue to adhere to the idea that spiritual realities must be dealt with prior to any permanent healing or legitimate cure.
29. Private interview with Nguyen family following traumatic experience in the hospital and misunderstanding with the resident staff.
30. Neal Palafox and Anne Warren, eds., *Cross-Cultural Caring: A*

Handbook for Health Care Professionals in Hawaii (Honolulu: Transcultural Health Care Forum, 1980).

31. Ibid., pp. 240–258.

32. Notes from a lecture by Dao The Xuong, Indochinese Refugee Resettlement Seminar, Oklahoma City, October 3, 1980.

33. Ibid.

34. Conversation with Dr. David Vu, Medical Doctor and Publisher of *Viet Bao,* Vietnamese language newspaper, Oklahoma City, 1988.

35. ORR, annual report, 1988.

36. Interviews in Denver of both Hispanic and Vietnamese persons gave similar descriptions of the actual events although the reasons behind those actions differed greatly.

37. Interviews in Seabrook, Houston and Galveston, Texas, with local fishermen, Vietnamese fishermen, and local business people. Also, *The Dallas Morning News* had articles on the difficulty in August 1979.

38. Donald N. Brown, *The Vietnamese-American Experience in Oklahoma* (Stillwater: College of Arts and Sciences, Oklahoma State University, 1981), pp. 4–5.

39. The interview was conducted by Bruce Harless, Vietnamese language missionary in Hawaii, 1990.

40. Letter from Bruce Harless, Vietnamese Pastor, University Baptist Church, Honolulu, Hawaii, December 23, 1989.

41. "Vietnamese Gangs in California," *Newsweek,* August 2, 1982, p. 22.

6. Personal Adjustments and Self-Identity

1. Conversation with Mr. Thu, Vietnamese-American Association, 1981. Information on the Vietnamese language was included on a sheet which he gave me, but which did not identify a source. Mr. Thu may have written the sheet himself or someone in the VAA could have prepared the material. It was distributed to sponsoring families who were not familiar with the Vietnamese language.

2. Charles Muzny, ESL instructor at the VAA, Oklahoma City, asked me to sit in his class in order that he might demonstrate that his students in the mid-level English class were still struggling with comprehension.

3. Charles H. Mindel, Robert W. Habenstein, and Roosevelt Wright, Jr., *Ethnic Families in America* (New York: Elsevier, 1988), p. 284.

4. Ibid., pp. 283–284.

5. Alfredo Capanto Bautista, "The Traditional Vietnamese Family in Transition: An Ethnographic Study" (Ph.D. dissertation), Ann Arbor: University Microfilms, 1983, p. 53.

6. 1980 Spring Survey, VAA, Oklahoma City.

7. "Asian Americans: Growth, Change, and Diversity," *Population Bulletin*, 1985, 40: 1–44.

8. Darrel Montero, *Vietnamese Americans: Patterns of Resettlement and Socioeconomic Adaptation in the United States* (Boulder: Westview Press, 1979).

9. Ibid., p. 1–44.

10. Conversation with Father Bao involving divorce among refugees and the pressures leading to marital break-ups.

11. Ibid., p. 292.

12. Ibid., p. 293–302.

13. Charles Muzny, "The Vietnamese in Oklahoma City: A Study of Ethnic Change" (Ph.D. dissertation, University of Oklahoma, 1985), p. 149.

14. Ibid., pp. 293–295.

15. Ibid., pp. 293–302.

16. Personal interviews conducted in several cities over a ten-year period.

17. Muzny, "Vietnamese in Oklahoma City," pp. 288–311.

18. "Historical Perspective on the Amerasian Issue," paper presented by Dao N. Spencer at Asian-American Conference, New York City, October 4–5, 1984. Published in a booklet by the American Council of Voluntary Agencies in Foreign Service, Committee on Migration and Refugee Affairs, p. 5.

19. Ibid., pp. 5–7.

20. *Refugee Reports*, 1989.

21. "Black Amerasians," *In America*, newsletter subtitled *Perspectives on Refugee Resettlement*, No. 4, June 1989, p. 3.

22. Sometimes the Amerasian is accompanied by the biological mother, sometimes by several persons, and other times by groups numbering from seven to ten persons.

23. *In America*, June 1989, pp. 1–4.

24. Têt is set according to the Lunar Calendar and in Vietnam was celebrated in strict observance to that calendar. In the United States, celebrations are in line with the calendar, but depending on the renting of public facilities, the public festivities may vary.

25. There is little or no question that to refugees, Têt remains the most important celebration.

26. Information obtained through the Diocese through a long-distance phone conversation, June 1990.

7. Contemporary Vietnamese-American Society

1. The Vietnamese Buddhist Temple is located at 857-863 Berendo Street, Los Angeles, California.

2. Vietnamese Buddhist Temple, *The Presence of Vietnamese Buddhists in America* (Los Angeles, 1981), p. 1.

3. "Vietnamese Raise Funds for Families," *The Daily Oklahoman*, no author cited, March 24, 1989, p. 15.

4. The September 1990 issue of the *St. Louis Magazine* provides interesting insights into Vietnamese refugees in one pocket of St. Louis.

5. Seth Mydans, "Vietnam War and Its Casualties Continue for Refugees in the US," *New York Times*, August 25, 1989, p. 29.

6. Paul Rutledge, "Traditional Patterns and Belief Orientations: The Prognosis for Vietnamese Acculturation and Assimilation in the United States," *Asian Journal of Theology*, Singapore, Spring 1988, pp. 516–545.

7. Ibid., pp. 531–537.

8. *The Bridge*, September 1988, p. 23.

9. Paul Rutledge, *The Vietnamese in America* (Minneapolis: Lerner Press, 1987), pp. 52–53.

10. Copy was obtained at the Cultural Center in Dallas, Texas.

11. Rutledge, *The Vietnamese in America*, pp. 52–53.

12. *Shawnee News-Star*, Thursday, November 17, 1988, p. 14A.

13. *Dallas Morning News*, May 28, 1981, p. 1A.

14. Paul Rutledge, *The Vietnamese in America* (Minneapolis: Lerner Press, 1987), pp. 52–53.

15. Paper presented by Dr. Jesse Nash at the Eighth Annual Information Transfer Meeting, The Minerals Management Service, Gulf of Mexico Region, New Orleans, December 1–3, 1987.

16. Ibid., p. 9.

SUGGESTIONS FOR
FURTHER READING

Aames, Jacqueline S., Ronald L. Aames, John Jung, and Edward Karabenick. *Indochinese Refugee Self-Sufficiency in California: A Survey and Analysis of the Vietnamese, Cambodians and Lao and the Agencies That Serve Them.* Report submitted to the State Department of Health, State of California, September 30, 1977.

Adler, Jerry. "The New Immigrants," *Newsweek*, July 7, 1980, pp. 26–31.

Anker, Deborah. *The Law of Asylum in the United States: A Manual for Practitioners and Adjudicators.* Washington, D.C.: American Immigration Lawyers Association, 1989.

Arden, Harvey. "Troubled Odyssey of Vietnamese Fishermen," *National Geographic*, September 1981, pp. 378–395.

Atkinson, Donald R., George Morten, and Derald Wing Sue. *Counseling American Minorities: A Cross-Cultural Perspective.* Dubuque, Iowa: Wm. C. Brown Publishers, 1979.

Aylesworth, Laurence S., Peter G. Ossorio, and Larry T. Osaki. "Stress and Mental Health Among Vietnamese in the United States," *Asian-Americans: Social and Psychological Perspectives.* Edited by R. Endo, S. Sue, and N. Wagner. Palo Alto, California: Basic Books, 1978.

Baker, Reginald P. and David S. North. *The 1975 Refugees: Their First Five Years in America.* Washington, D.C.: New TransCentury Foundation, 1984.

Barger, W. K., and Tham V. Truong. "Community Action Work Among the Vietnamese," *Human Organization*, Vol. 37, No. 1, Spring 1978, pp. 95–100.

Barth, Fredrik, ed. *Ethnic Groups and Boundaries: The Social Organization of Culture Differences.* Oslo, Norway: Bergen, 1969.

Bennoun, Phillip, Robert Bennoun, and Paula Kelly. *The Peoples from Indo-China.* Victoria, Australia: Hodja Educational Resources Cooperative, 1984.

Berry, John W. "Acculturation as Varieties of Adaption—," *Acculturation: Theory, Models and Some New Findings.* Edited by Arnado Padilla. Boulder, Colorado: Westview Press, 1980.

Boosey, Anne, et al. *A Comparative Study of Relocated Vietnamese in Rural and Urban Arkansas.* Little Rock: Arkansas University, 1976.

Brown, Donald N. *The Vietnamese-American Experience in Oklahoma.* Stillwater: Oklahoma State University, College of Arts and Sciences Extension, 1981.

Burling, Robbins. *Hill Farms and Padi Fields: Life in Mainland Southeast Asia.* Englewood Cliffs, New Jersey: Prentice-Hall, 1965.

California Department of Social Services. *Indochinese Refugee Assistance Program: Characteristics Survey.* Sacramento, California: Statistical Services Bureau. Department of Social Services. Health and Welfare Agency, April 1980.

——. *The Assimilation and Acculturation of Indochinese Children into American Culture.* Sacramento: Department of Social Services. Health and Welfare Agency, August, 1980.

Caplan, Nathan, John K. Whitmore, and Marcella H. Choy. *The Boat People and Achievement in America: A Study of Family Life, Hard Work and Cultural Values.* Ann Arbor: University of Michigan Press, 1989.

Cartmail, Keith St. *Exodus Indochina.* Surrey, England: Heinemann Publishers, 1983.

Center for Applied Linguistics. *Education in Vietnam: Fundamental Principles and Curricula.* Arlington, Virginia: Center for Applied Linguistics, n.d.

——. *On Assimilating Vietnamese and Cambodian Students into United States Schools.* Arlington, Virginia: Center for Applied Linguistics, n.d.

——. *Vietnamese History, Literature and Folklore.* Arlington, Virginia: Center for Applied Linguistics, n.d.

Chantavanich, Supang and E. Bruce Reynolds, *Indochinese Refugees: Asylum and Resettlement.* Bangkok: Institute of Asian Studies, Chulalongkorn University, 1988.

Chaze, William L. "Refugees, Stung by a Backlash," *U.S. News and World Report,* October 13, 1980, pp. 60–63.

Chu, Judy May. *The Psychological Adjustment Process of the Vietnamese Refugees.* Los Angeles: California School of Professional Psychology, 1979.

Caides, G. *The Making of South East Asia.* Berkeley: University of California Press, 1966.

——. *The Indianized States of Southeast Asia.* Honolulu: University Press of Hawaii, 1971.

Dean, Vera Micheles. *The Nature of the Non-Western World.* New York: Mentor Books, 1966.

Despres, Leo A., ed. *Ethnicity and Resource Competition in Plural Societies.* The Hague: Mouton Publishing, 1975.

Dinnerstein, Leonard, and David Reimers. *Ethnic Americans: A History of Immigration and Assimilation.* New York: Dodd, Mead & Company, 1975.

Dinnerstein, Leonard, Roger Nichols, and David Reimers. *Natives and Strangers: Ethnic Groups and the Building of America.* New York: Oxford University Press, 1979.

Doan, Han T. *Factors That Foster or Impede the Process of Acculturation of Vietnamese Refugees.* Provo, Utah: Brigham Young University, 1977.

Dorais, Louis-Jacques, Lise Pilon-Le, and Nguyen Huy. *Exile in a Cold Land: A Vietnamese Community in Canada.* New Haven: Southeast Asian Studies, Yale University, 1987.

FitzGerald, Frances. *Fire in the Lake: The Vietnamese and the Americans in Vietnam.* Boston: Little, Brown, 1972.

Freeman, James M. *Hearts of Sorrow: Vietnamese-American Lives.* Stanford, California: Stanford University Press, 1989.

Garcia, Eduardo, and Bernard R. Snow. *Southeast Asian Refugees in Philadelphia.* Philadelphia: Department of Public Welfare, 1986.

Geertz, Clifford. *The Interpretation of Cultures.* New York: Basic Books, 1973.

Gim, Wever, and Tybel Litwin. *Indochinese Refugees in America: Profiles of Five Communities.* U.S. Department of State. Executive Seminar in National and International Affairs, April 1980.

Glazer, Nathan, ed. *Clamor at the Gates: The New American Immigration.* San Francisco: Institute for Contemporary Studies, 1985.

Gozdziak, Elzbieta. *Older Refugees in the United States: From Dignity to Despair.* Washington, D.C.: Refugee Policy Group, 1988.

Gordon, Linda W. "Settlement Patterns of Indochinese Refugees in the United States." U.S. Department of Justice: Immigration and Naturalization Service. *INS Reporter,* Vol. 28, No. 3, Spring 1980, pp. 6–10.

Haines, David, Dorothy Rutherford, and Patrick Thomas. "Family and Community Among Vietnamese Refugees," *International Migration Review,* Vol. 15, No. 1, Spring 1981.

Harrell-Bond, B. E. *Imposing Aid: Emergency Assistance to Refugees.* Oxford: Oxford University Press, 1986.

Ha Ton Vinh. "Indochinese Mutual Assistance Associations," *Journal of Refugee Resettlement,* Vol. 1, No. 1, November 1980, pp. 49–52.

Haskins, James. *The New Americans: Vietnamese Boat People.* Hillside, New Jersey: Enslow Publishers, 1980.

Hawthorne, Lesleyanne, ed. *Refugee: The Vietnamese Experience.* Oxford: Oxford University Press, 1982.

Hearn, Robert M. *Thai Government Programs in Refugee Relocation and Resettlement in Northern Thailand.* Auburn, New York: Thailand Books, 1974.

Hickey, Gerald Cannon. *Village in Vietnam.* New Haven: Yale University Press, 1964.

Horn, Jack C. "Vietnamese Immigrants: Doing Poorly by Doing Well," *Psychology Today*, June 1980, pp. 103–104.

Haskins, Marilyn and Eleanor Shepherd. *Life in a Vietnamese Urban Quarter*. Southern Illinois University, Center for Vietnamese Studies, Carbondale, Monograph No. 1, 1966.

Hundley, Norris, Jr., ed. *The Asian American: The Historical Experience*. Santa Barbara, California: Clio Books, 1976.

Institute of Asian Studies. *Thailand: A First Asylum Country for Indochinese Refugees*. Bangkok: Chulalongkorn University, Asian Monographs, No. 38, 1988.

Kalupahana, David J. *Buddhist Philosophy: A Historical Analysis*. Honolulu: University Press of Hawaii, 1976.

Kelly, Gail Paradise. *From Vietnam to America: A Chronicle of the Vietnamese Immigration to the United States*. Boulder, Colorado: Westview Press, 1977.

Khoa, Le Xuan. "Vietnamese Immigrants and Their Adjustment to American Society," *Dat Moi* Newspaper, Seattle, Washington, September 1981.

Khoa, Le Xuan, and John Vandeusen. "Social and Cultural Customs: Their Contribution to Resettlement," *Journal of Refugee Resettlement*, Vol. 1, No. 2, March 1981, pp. 48–52.

Knoll, Tricia. *Becoming Americans: Asian Sojourners, Immigrants, and Refugees in the Western United States*. Portland, Oregon: Coast to Coast Books, 1982.

Knudsen, John C. *Boat People in Transit: Vietnamese in Refugee Camps in the Philippines, Hong Kong and Japan*. Bergen, Norway: Occasional Papers in Social Anthropology, 1983.

Krupinski, J. and G. Burrows, eds. *The Price of Freedom: Young Indochinese Refugees in Australia*. Sydney, Australia: Pergamon Press, 1986.

Lawyers Committee For Human Rights. *Refuge Denied: Problems in the Protection of Vietnamese and Cambodians in Thailand and the Admission of Indochinese Refugees in to the United States*. New York: Lawyers Committee for Human Rights, 1989.

Lester, Robert C. *Theravada Buddhism in Southeast Asia*. Ann Arbor: University of Michigan Press, 1973.

Lewins, Frank and Judith Ly. *The First Wave: The Settlement of Australia's First Vietnamese Refugees*. North Sydney, Australia: George Allen & Unwin, 1985.

Liu, William T. *Transition to Nowhere: Vietnamese Refugees in America*. Nashville, Tennessee: Charter House, 1979.

Loescher, Gil and John A. Scanlan. *Calculated Kindness: Refugees and America's Half-Open Door, 1945 to the Present*. New York: Free Press, 1986.

Maclear, Michael. *The Ten Thousand Day War, Vietnam: 1945–1975*. New York: St. Martin's Press, 1981.

Maril, Robert Lee. *Texas Shrimpers: Community, Capitalism, and the Sea*. College Station: Texas A&M University Press, 1983.

Miserez, Diana, ed. *Refugees: The Trauma of Exile*. Netherlands: Martinus Nijhoff Publishers, 1988.

Montero, Darrel. *Vietnamese Americans: Patterns of Resettlement and Socioeconomic Adaptation in the United States*. Boulder, Colorado: Westview Press, 1979.

Nash, Jesse. *Vietnamese Values: Confucian, Catholic, American*. Ann Arbor: University Microfilms International, 1987.

Nash, Manning. *Anthropological Studies in Theravada Buddhism*. Yale University Southeast Asia Studies, Cultural Report Series, No. 13, 1966.

Nguyen, Dinh-Hoa, ed. *Some Aspects of Vietnamese Culture*. Carbondale: Center for Vietnamese Studies, University of Southern Illinois, 1972.

Nguyen-Hong-Nhiem, Lucy and Joel Martin Halpern, eds. *The Far East Comes Near: Autobiographical Accounts of Southeast and Asian Students in America*. Amherst: University of Massachusetts, 1989.

Nguyen-Hy Quang. *Perspectives on a Cross-Cultural Problem: Getting to Know the Vietnamese*. Arlington, Virginia: Center for Applied Linguistics, 1975.

Nguyen, Xuan Thu, and Desmond Cahill. *Understanding Vietnamese Refugees in Australia*. Coburg, Australia: Phillip Institute of Technology, 1986.

Oggeri, Lechi Tran. *The Unique Characteristics of the Vietnamese Culture That Affect the Process of Adjustment of Vietnamese Refugees to American Culture*. Raleigh: North Carolina State University, 1979.

Oliver, Victor L. *Caodai Spiritism: A Study of Religion in Vietnamese Society*. Leiden, Netherlands: E. J. Brill, 1976.

Opportunity Systems, Inc. *First Wave Report, Vietnam Resettlement Operational Feedback*. Washington, D.C.: Opportunity Systems, Contract No. HEW-100-76-0042, October 2, 1975.

―――. *Second Wave Report, Vietnam Resettlement Operational Feedback*. Washington, D.C.: Opportunity Systems, January 1976.

Poole, Peter A. *The Vietnamese in Thailand: A Historical Perspective*. Ithaca: Cornell University Press, 1970.

Popkin, Samuel L. *The Rational Peasant: The Political Economy of Rural Society in Vietnam*. Berkeley: University of California Press, 1979.

Purcell, Victor. *The Chinese in Southeast Asia*. New York: Oxford University Press, 1951.

Rogge, John, ed. *Refugees: A Third World Dilemma*. Totowa, New Jersey: Rowman & Littlefield, 1987.

Royce, Anya Peterson. *Ethnic Identity*. Bloomington: Indiana University Press, 1982.

Rutledge, Paul. "The Vietnamese-Americans of Oklahoma," *Vietnam Forum*, Yale University Southeast Asia Studies Journal, New Haven, Connecticut, Vol. 2, Summer-Fall, 1983.
———. *The Role of Religion in Ethnic Self-Identity: A Vietnamese Community*. Lanham, Maryland: University Press of America, 1985.
Simon, Julian L. *How Do Immigrants Affect US Economically?* Washington, D.C.: Center for Immigration Policy and Refugee Assistance, Georgetown University, 1985.
Simon, Walter B. *Cultural Identity Between Assimilation and Tradition*. Vienna: Soziologisches Institute, University of Vienna, 1978.
Smith, Ralph. "Religion," *Viet-Nam and the West*. Ithaca: New York: Cornell University Press, 1971.
Smith, R. B. "The Cycle of Confucianization in Vietnam," *Aspects of Vietnamese History*. Honolulu: University Press of Hawaii, 1973, pp. 1–29.
Starr, Paul D. "Troubled Waters: Vietnamese Fisherfolk on America's Gulf Coast," *International Migration Review*, Vol. 15, No. 1, Spring-Summer 1981, pp. 226–238.
Stein, Howard F. and Robert F. Hill. *The Ethnic Imperative*. University Park: Pennsylvania State University Press, 1977.
Steinfield, Melvin. *Cracks in the Melting Pot: Racism and Discrimination in American History*. Beverly Hills, California: Glencoe Press, 1970.
Strand, Paul and Woodrow Jones, Jr. *Indochinese Refugees in America: Problems of Adaptation and Assimilation*. Durham, North Carolina: Duke University Press, 1985.
Sutter, Valerie O'Conner. *The Indo-Chinese Refugee Dilemma*. Baton Rouge: Louisiana State University Press, 1990.
Taniwaki, Marge Yamada, et al. "Denver's Westside Community: The Impact of Indochinese Resettlement on a Predominantly Chicano Neighborhood," *Proceedings of the First Annual Conference on Indochinese Refugees*. Compiled by G. Harry Stopp, Jr. and Nguyen Mang Hung. Fairfax, Virginia: George Mason University, October 1979.
Tepper, Elliot L., ed. *Southeast Asian Exodus: From Tradition to Resettlement, Understanding Refugees from Laos, Kampuchea, and Vietnam in Canada*. Ottawa: Canadian Asian Studies Association, 1980.
Thuy, Vuong G. *Getting to Know the Vietnamese and Their Culture*. New York: Frederick Ungar, 1976.
Tsamenyi, B. Martin. "The 'Boat People': Are They Refugees?" *Human Rights Quarterly*, Baltimore: Johns Hopkins University Press. Vol. 5, No. 3, August 1983.
———. House of Representatives. Committee on the Judiciary. Subcommittee on Immigration, Refugees, and International Law.

Refugee Act of 1979: Hearings before the Subcommittee on Immigration, Refugees, and International Law. 96th Congress, 1st Session. Washington, D.C., May 1979.

U.S. Department of Health, Education, and Welfare. *HEW Refugee Task Force. Report to the Congress.* Washington, D.C.: U.S. DHEW, March 15, 1976–December 31, 1977.

U.S. General Accounting Office. *The Indochinese Exodus: A Humanitarian Dilemma: Report to the Congress.* By the Comptroller General of the United States. Washington, D.C., April 24, 1979.

Viviana, Nancy. *The Long Journey: Vietnamese Migration and Resettlement in Australia.* Melbourne, Australia: Melbourne University Press, 1984.

Von der Mehden, Fred. *The Ethnic Groups of Houston.* Houston: Rice University Press, 1984.

Ward, Martha, and Zachary Gussow. "The Vietnamese in New Orleans: A Preliminary Report," *Perspectives on Ethnicity in New Orleans.* New Orleans: University of New Orleans Press, 1979.

Whitefield, Danny J. *Historical and Cultural Dictionary of Vietnam.* Metuchen, New Jersey: Scarecrow Press, 1976.

Zolberg, Aristotle, Astri Suhrke, and Sergio Aguayo. *Escape from Violence: Conflict and the Refugee Crisis in the World.* Oxford: Oxford University Press, 1989.

INDEX

Adolescents:
  adjustment of, 61
  as viewed by parents, 104,
    118
  language acquisition, 115
  becoming American, 122–123
  at risk, 128–129
  and Têt, 137–138
Amerasians:
  category of, 65–66
  history of, 132–133
  resettlement of, 133–135
  acceptance of, 134–136
Asylum:
  countries of first, 11–12
  countries of second, 12–13
Asylum seekers:
  definition of, 7

Boat people:
  movements of, 14
  defined, 62–63
Buddhism:
  temple in Oklahoma City, 43,
    141–142, 151
  introduced to Vietnam, 47
  features of, 47–48
  acceptance in Port Arthur, 50–
    51
  adaptations of, 50–53
  conflict with city council, 110–
    111
  conflict with Catholicism, 110–
    112
  expression of, 140–141
  in Beaumont, Texas, 141–142

Chinese:
  ethnic population, 7
  boat people, 63
Confucianism:
  features of, 48–49
Customs:
  family, 116–119
  Têt, 136–138

Education:
  first wave, 3–4
  honored place of, 89
  cultural influence of Chinese,
    89–90
  under the French, 90–91
  for adults, 93
  concerning culture, 141
  success of, 148

Family:
  precedence of, 83
  customs concerning, 116–119
  characteristics of, 119–121
  economics of, 121–123
  gender role change, 123–126
  changing roles within, 123–129
  courtship and marriage, 129–
    132

Gangs:
  ethnic Vietnamese, 110–112

Health Care:
  problems with, 98
  cultural values pertaining to,
    98–102
  supernatural cause of illness,
    99–101
  mental health, 103–106
Housing:
  initial, 96–98
  conflict with, 106–109

Immigrants:
  definition of, 7–8

Kailua Baptist Church, Hawaii:
  reception of refugees, 40–42
Khmer:
  minority in Southeast Asia, 5–6
  movements of, 14
Khmer Rouge:
  in Cambodia, 1
  attack on refugees, 16

172

PAUL JAMES RUTLEDGE is Associate Professor of Anthropology and a Fellow, Center for International Studies at the University of Missouri–St. Louis.